COMING HOME TO SICILY

SICILY

Seasonal Harvests and Cooking from Case Vecchie

FABRIZIA LANZA *with Kate Winslow*

Foreword by ALICE WATERS

Photography by GUY AMBROSINO

VALLELUNGA →

REGALEALI →

CASE VECCHIE
punto vendita   →

Foreword   viii
Introduction   xi

Winter 1

Spring 83

Summer 143

Fall 215

Epilogue 297
Sources 300
Acknowledgments 303
Index 304

FOREWORD

The first time I visited Anna Tasca Lanza's cooking school was for my fifty-first birthday, in 1995, with my friend Mary Taylor Simeti. I remember the hour and a half drive up the winding hills to Regaleali, through some of the most beautiful landscape imaginable. It was breathtaking: The tangles of wild fennel along the roadsides, the rolling hills, the gnarled grapevines—as we drove through the Sicilian countryside, it felt as though we were traveling back to another time bristling with color and wildness and life. And there, as we crested a hill, the old stone buildings of the estate came into view—right in the heart of it all. We were welcomed like family.

In my memory the place is, of course, inextricably linked to the dishes that Anna and her family had been creating for generations. She maintained a lush kitchen garden from which she would snip rosemary and mint and parsley as she cooked. Every meal we ate was perfectly of that place, deeply grounded in the rugged land that surrounded us. We stayed in the guest house next to the courtyard, where the students at the cooking school baked loaves of rustic bread in the wood oven (the wheat had been harvested from the surrounding fields), and where they produced pecorino and ricotta from the milk of the Case Vecchie's resident sheep. I remember that on my birthday Anna made cream puffs filled with a heavenly fresh cream that just tumbled out of them. They were simple and profoundly satisfying—I have tried to replicate them on many occasions, but they never taste quite as divine as they did upon that first tasting. It must be the cream—or more precisely, what the animals are eating up there.

It was springtime when I arrived, and Anna would take me on walks through the countryside to show me the wildflowers. You couldn't take a single step without encountering a new wild herb—amazingly, she knew the name of every single plant. I remember how quiet it was, walking through the hills with the blue sky and big billowy white clouds above.

Over the years, I've had the opportunity to experience the magic of Regaleali a handful of times, and came to know and love both Anna and her wonderful daughter Fabrizia. One of the things I left with on one of my visits was a little picture booklet on how to make sun-dried tomato paste—*estratto*—the way Sicilians have been making it for centuries. They would put the fruit in giant vats and cook it over an open fire, and after the mixture had reduced, the tomato paste was spread on tables in the courtyard to bake in the hot sun. As the tomatoes dried over the course of several days, they would be scraped down into smaller and smaller heaps. Each time I left the school with a little jar of the final paste—it has a flavor so intense, you only need a quarter teaspoon of it in a pasta to evoke the essence of Sicily. How thrilled I was, then, to discover this very process—the great big pots of boiling tomatoes, the courtyard filled with table upon table of vivid red *estratto*—lovingly photographed and described here in Fabrizia's book. This celebration of tradition continues to amaze and inspire me.

It was, and is, so clear to me that this is a place for deep edible education, reaching out to visitors through all the senses: touch, taste, smell, sound, sight. How lucky we are, then, that Fabrizia has so fearlessly stepped into Anna's shoes, embodying the values of her mother and the property and carrying on the legacy of the school with such grace and passion. This is a quality about Fabrizia I very much admire; she sees the world around her with the eye of an historian, the layers and the tradition and the art that are built into everything she creates in her kitchen. She knows these recipes in her bones, believes in the purity and provenance of the ingredients, and teaches visitors from around the world with effortlessness and charm. All this is so beautifully represented in these pages: Simple, seasonal, robust dishes that appeal on a fundamental level and reveal the generosity of spirit that Fabrizia has in such abundance.

— *Alice Waters*

INTRODUCTION

When people ask me if I learned to cook from my mother, I feel a bit odd saying no. Neither my mother nor I grew up with any real cooking experience. After all, my family belonged to the Sicilian aristocracy, and we were privileged enough to have wonderful cooks—Totò and Agostina at our house and Mario at my grandparents' villa—who took care of all our meals. So there is no pretty, romantic picture of me learning how to make pastry dough at my mother's elbow. When I was young, my mother was rarely in the kitchen, but I spent many an evening there, teasing and playing with Totò while waiting for my mother, beautifully dressed and covered in jewels, to sweep in and visit me before she went out. She reminded me of a lioness, coming to pet her cub before going out into the wilds of cocktails and dancing!

And yet, my mother, Anna Tasca Lanza, went on to become known as the queen of Sicilian cuisine, and I have found myself following in her footsteps, carrying on the tradition of the cooking school she started on our family's estate in the middle of the island. How could this be?

Basically, my mother and I both learned how to cook by eating. I have always been an enthusiastic omnivore, what in Italy we call *una buona forchetta*—a "good fork"—and I was especially fortunate to enjoy a wealth of eating experiences, both high and low, from a young age. I lived with my parents in a villa in the seaside town of Mondello, on the outskirts of Palermo. Every morning, I went to a public school in the city. Outside of the school, there were plenty of vendors selling *sfincione* and *panelle*, which secured me a good apprenticeship, if you will, in Sicilian street food. But when I came home for lunch, I would find the dining table set with *poule au riz*, egg ribbons, gazpacho, and chicken liver fricassee, which guaranteed another horizon of knowledge.

SICILY

My childhood was greatly influenced by my two grandfathers, who were both grand gourmets; but even between the two sides of my family, the Lanzas and the Tascas, there were substantial differences in cooking styles and preferences. My paternal grandfather, Fabrizio Lanza, for whom I am named, was very cosmopolitan. He grew up in Rome, married a Spanish lady, my grandmother Conchita, who truly did not know how to boil an egg, and preferred French cuisine above all else (except for spaghetti with *ragù alla bolognese*, which he craved).

My maternal grandfather, Giuseppe Tasca, was much more local. He lived in Sicily his whole life and married one of the wittiest, sportiest young girls from Palermo, my grandmother Franca, who loved food as much as he did (though she spent her whole life pretending she was on a diet). When I was a child, they lived part of the winter in an ornate villa in Palermo and divided the rest of the year between a house in Mondello, just down the street from us, and Regaleali.

This fertile swath of land in the interior of Sicily, about ninety minutes from Palermo, has been in the family for nearly two hundred years. The property had two great old stone homes built around cobblestoned courtyards, acres and acres of grapevines, olive trees, fruit trees, and vegetable gardens, plus dozens of sheep that provided all the ricotta and pecorino the family could eat. Giuseppe and Franca made their home at Case Grandi, the larger house, built high on a hill that overlooked almost the entire property. The smaller house, Case Vecchie, was eventually passed down to my mother. My grandfather loved French cuisine, but he was equally thrilled by all the extraordinary fresh produce that came every day from the estate, and he knew a lot about Sicilian traditions. With his chef Mario's imposing Franco/Sicilian background and assistance, he made sure that things like *panelle* had a place at our family's table next to more vaunted dishes. And, of course, there was the wine. Grapes had always been grown at Regaleali, but my grandfather set out to make a wine that could stand up to a great Bordeaux. His first great success was the Rosso del Conte, a strong, full-bodied red made from Sicily's native grape, Nero d'Avola. Indeed, there was much to taste and to learn for a curious child like me.

But for understandable reasons, I had to make my own life outside of this big challenging family. At the age of eighteen, I left Sicily for France and, later, the north of Italy to study art history, and after I finished school, I stayed there. Food was definitely not my primary interest at this time, and I lived happily on salads and cheese. Plus, about every six months, I received a treasure trove of goods from Regaleali—bottles of homemade tomato sauce, wine, olive oil, marmalades, canned tuna, dried herbs, sun-dried tomatoes—lovingly organized by my grandmother Franca. These shipments would round out my friends' and my meals for the next little while. Eventually, I became a full-time museum curator and art historian in the Veneto region, married, and had two children. My life in the north wasn't easy, but I was independent. Sicily is really another world from the rest of Italy, with a different mentality. Because of my background, life in Sicily may have been comfortable and privileged, but I could never escape the family and history I was born into. For the next twenty-five years, I returned to Sicily only for holidays.

Meanwhile, my mother was finding her own way. My life was incredibly free and full of choices compared to my mother's early years. She was brought up to look beautiful, to marry well, and to have lots of kids. She succeeded at the first two, but I was her only child. She was certainly not expected to work, let alone become an entrepreneur. Looking at her younger self, it seems almost impossible that my mother would go on to start a renowned cooking school. But she was in many ways extraordinarily curious, full of life, and far too intelligent to limit herself to being only a wife and mother.

The cooking school started as a bit of a lark. My mother had a gift for handcrafts, and she knitted dozens of elaborate sweaters, then moved on to bookbinding, before finally making her way to cooking. She had just restored Case Vecchie and saw that opening part of it as a cooking school could be a way to stay close to her beloved parents. She asked her sisters, Rosemarie and Costanza, to join her, and Mario was there to mentor her first classes. The cooking school was born in 1989. No one really paid much attention to it, least of all my mother, and she was truly surprised when the first group of students showed up. She started traveling to big culinary conventions in the United States and found that people knew little about Sicily—except what they'd seen in *The Godfather*—which was very frustrating in the beginning.

Mario didn't stay with the school for very long. He was very secretive about his recipes, while my mother's palate was leading her away from haute cuisine and toward more simple, traditional Sicilian food, especially wild vegetables. My mother never did anything halfway; things had to be genuine. I remember my father's face when she presented him with a platter of spaghetti simply covered with wild greens and no sauce or seasoning except a spoonful of olive oil. He had been brought up on the most sophisticated French cuisine of the 1920s, dishes based on eggs, béchamel, butter, and cream, and he looked quite desperate!

When my mother's first book, *The Heart of Sicily,* was published, it embodied a certain transition between the "old-fashioned" cuisine that Sicilian aristocrats and wealthy families had eaten up until the 1980s and the new interest in light, healthy, "peasant" cooking. In fact, the timing was perfect—Mediterranean cuisine was ravishing the world, the switch from French to Italian was in the air, and olive oil was all the rage. Therefore, people from all over the world started coming to the school, and because there was no competition, things grew quickly.

As for myself, I had moved beyond my diet of salads and cheese. My husband, Luca, and I were living in Verona with our children, Ruggero and Virginia. I was curious, and there was plenty to learn there—lots of polentas and stews and rich, unforgettable flavors. And because my mother was now established with the cooking school, I could call on her for advice. (I see the same thing now happening with Virginia and me!) I was getting to be a good cook, simply by tasting and experimenting and asking questions. Every time I prepared a fancy meal, Luca would laughingly say, "When are you going to stop this art history nonsense and just cook?!?" But my identity was wrapped up in my museum work, not the kitchen. It was only much later—after both my marriage and job ended, and when my mother asked me to help her with the school—that I realized I was finally ready to untangle some of the knots I had with my family roots. So, at the age of forty-five, I returned to Sicily.

Coming home was difficult at first. My mother loved me with all the passion one can think of, but she was a very strong woman and wanted me to follow her lead. How dare I act or think differently than she did?! This had long been a problem, and so I had gone away, and stayed away. I stepped into her world very gradually, first accompanying her on promotional trips. We went to the U.S. together, and she introduced me to her friends in the culinary world. We also traveled to Malta, the U.K., and India, and I began assisting her with classes at Case Vecchie, as well.

I moved from my first life as an art historian and curator to my new life as a chef and instructor without any real despair or lack of confidence, a trait I certainly inherited from my mother. I realized that learning how to make a cassata was no less interesting than analyzing a Botticelli. I consider both to be works of art. So after nearly thirty years of art history, I transferred that same level of passion to cooking, and I could not get enough! I started by working in my mother's footsteps, but soon I was adjusting, comparing, introducing new ingredients, and inventing recipes as I explored my own pleasures and tastes. I also started interviewing villagers and filming them while they kneaded dough or prepared feast day recipes. Sicily offers such a wide and amazing scene for cooking, raw ingredients, and traditions that it seems I don't need to move anywhere else to feed my endless curiosity. I have been trying to organize the unconscious know-how my mother placed in my hands and provide a deeper awareness of how important it is to preserve these ancient processes and methods. It was, and still is, challenging and hugely exciting.

Splitting my time between Palermo and Case Vecchie, I was also rediscovering myself and my home. I was unexpectedly and completely overwhelmed by the pleasure of finding my senses again. Flavors, lights, temperatures, rumors, silences, nature, colors, smiles, looks, landscapes, warmth . . . these particular impressions of Sicily all came flooding back to me. Certain foods, like zucchini soup with *tenerumi*, which you can only find in Sicily, propelled me back into memories; but so did words, hand gestures, noises, smells, the very air brushing against my skin. I loved the decadence of taking a lazy hike through wild oregano fields with a friend and catching the last breeze from the ocean at night while eating sparkling fresh seafood. I fell back into the Sicilian habit of quarreling loudly with other drivers over a parking spot. I slipped into the natural rhythm of making marmalade in the winter, canning tuna in the spring, jarring tomato sauce in the summer, and preparing quince paste as the air cooled in the fall. I hadn't realized how much I had missed all this while I was away, and I was surprised by how happy I was to be back—and to claim food as the core of my life.

It was during a promotional trip to India that I first noticed that my mother did not seem like herself. She was tired and insecure, no longer the lioness I knew from my childhood. Something was wrong, but it would be two long years before we figured out what. My mother was fading away, and we were both in trouble. She wouldn't let go, and I had to figure out a way to take over her work without threatening her. When she was finally diagnosed with Parkinson's disease in 2009, I could finally step in and take care of her. But still, it wasn't easy. I think she had mixed feelings about passing the command of her own creature—the cooking school—to me. But, despite these conflicts, we unexpectedly became very close. When she needed help, I was there for her and extraordinarily happy and proud to be useful.

I started cooking for my mother, something very new for both of us. In the beginning, she could be very suspicious, but I instinctively knew what she wanted: puréed chard with poached eggs, capellini in broth with ricotta, pasta with tomato sauce, marinated fish, lots of ice creams, lemon cream, *taralli*, crème caramel. . . . The last thing I made for her was a lemon granita. By that point, she had stopped talking and couldn't open her eyes, but she tasted a spoonful of the tart, icy granita and, in a whisper, said, "Squisito!" She passed away a few days later, on July 12, 2010.

In the months since then, as I have worked to honor my mother's legacy while also making my own mark on the cooking school, I have thought a lot about what I have learned from her, what legacy she has left me. I no doubt got my enthusiasm for life and open-minded curiosity from my mother, but she also left me something more tangible. I have some old Polaroids framed at Case Vecchie that show the property before my mother planted the garden that now lies below the house. From those little photographs, you can tell that my mother managed to transform a little patch of desert into an Eden. Now that I am looking after her garden—as it gradually becomes my garden—whenever I plant an orange or lemon or walnut sapling I realize that I shall have to wait two or ten or even twenty years before I see it as a tree. This thought makes me immensely grateful for my mother's foresight and patience. The trees she planted so many years ago now produce not only fruit but cool patches of shade, which are so precious in this warm, sunny climate.

I remember my mother telling me that she didn't like planting trees that didn't produce something edible. Today we would say she had a vision about eating locally—as Slow Food founder Carlo Petrini would say, kilometer zero—but I actually think it wasn't so much a vision as just what she knew. It was her soul. She had grown up at Regaleali, with the sights and the smells of the old orchards, the old processes, the old rhythms, so I don't think she was aiming for ideas that would later become trendy and current; she was simply going back to those practical, proven ways of doing things.

My mother passed these roots to me, but obviously I denied them as long as I could. Those roots were too heavy to carry, and I had to make my own way without them. But then, once I came back, I realized I was in fact on the same path as my mother, one that looked both backward and forward.

So much has changed since my mother started the cooking school so many years ago. The understanding of Sicily and its culture has evolved greatly over the past decades. *The Godfather* stereotype no longer dominates. Instead, Sicily seems to have found a place in the collective imagination as a kind of reservoir of tastes and traditions that have been lost in other places. I think of it as the last of the western countries and the first of the eastern ones.

Likewise, the school's early guests were mostly Italian Americans looking for a trace of their roots. Now, the variety of guests is much more diverse, and they come not only from the U.S., but Brazil, Australia, New Zealand, and all over Europe, and their approach to food is quite different. It is no longer a matter of finding one's Italian heritage, or even just eating marvelous food and drinking good wines. A visit to Case Vecchie is a chance to experience where the food comes from and how it is handled as it is processed and preserved. The harvesting of herbs and wild greens, the making of marmalades and liqueurs—I have opened these beautiful practices to my guests and invite them to participate. Guests are as enthusiastic—if not more so—to watch a shepherd make fresh ricotta or help out with our marmalade-making as they are to sit down to a fine meal. People want to know the story behind the food, and they want to know how to make things from scratch.

So many of us want to feel some responsibility for what we eat, and the best way to do so is to follow the whole path from the beginning, to know where our fruits, vegetables, meats, and milk come from, and then to have a hand in preserving them. Since coming home to Sicily, I have felt the sun's heat on my neck while I stirred tomato paste in the courtyard, and I have crawled up the hills, hunting for wild fennel, and the dishes I have cooked with these ingredients have tasted all the sweeter for those experiences. Ricotta, vinegar, vino cotto, *estratto*, tomato sauce, cured olives, quince paste, dried herbs, preserved artichokes, candied orange peel, marmalades . . . these are all things we make during the year at Case Vecchie. These processes are described in the following pages, but I hope that what they convey is not just a collection of recipes, but a way of living, not just a how-to, but an inspiration.

Fabrizia Lanza

WINTER

Winter in the interior of Sicily can be mean—windy, cold, even freezing. I often wake up to find the mountains surrounding Regaleali covered with snow and villages like Sclafani obscured by fog. The valleys between the tidy grapevines are sludged with frost, and the gnarled brown vines are bare.

But all is forgiven as soon as the sun comes out. The sky turns a bright, deep blue and the grayness of the fields disappears, replaced by scarves of emerald and jade green—these are the wheat fields that climb up and down the hills, and the wild greens that pop up along the verge of the roads. I am always captivated by the health of the land at this time of year, especially compared to June when the grasses have turned to straw. Now, the soil is luxurious, wealthy, and inviting.

We are months away from the roasting heat of the summer, so this is a great time to prune and feed the roses and fruit trees and start the long work of preparing the grapevines for the season. From December to February, the hills buzz with the workers embarking on the *pota secca*. Working in small groups, the men check each vine and carefully cut off all the old woody branches, keeping only the few that will carry the future fruits. Then, from April to June, when the vines start to awaken after the freeze and shoot out branches, the men rush madly from one vineyard to another, working to prevent the vines from leafing out too quickly. This "green pruning" (*pota verde*) helps the vine channel all her strength into the remaining branches that will carry the grapes. Limiting the amount of fruit grown on each vine not only intensifies the grapes' flavor, it helps the fruit grow stronger and become more resistant to disease, which can come with summer's intense heat and humidity.

CITRUS

Winter is the citrus moment in Sicily. We are literally surrounded by oranges, lemons, tangerines, grapefruit, kumquats, and citrons. The orange tree is our natural Christmas tree! Not surprisingly the Sicilian word for "garden"—*giardino*—actually means citrus garden. The whole island is covered with citruses from Christmas until the end of April, when the last tangerines, the Tardivo di Ciaculli, and blood oranges such as Tarocco and Moro, are harvested.

Even though lemons and oranges are available nearly all year long, there's no question that winter is the best season for them. The idea is to preserve as much as we can now so we can enjoy that fresh citrus scent and flavor for the rest of the year. The cooking school is slow during winter, but Giovanna, the housekeeper at Case Vecchie, and I are busy in the kitchen, making candied orange peel and putting up jar upon jar of preserves. For a few weeks during the winter, perfumes of tangerine, orange, and lemon waft through the kitchen's narrow windows and invade the courtyard. It reminds me of the witch's house in Hansel and Gretel!

Our marmalades are enjoyed in many ways—we serve them with toast, we line the bottoms of crostatas with marmalade and top them with fresh fruit, and sometimes we place a dollop in the bottom of a glass and then spoon Biancomangiare (page 88) over it.

My first time making citrus preserves in Case Vecchie's kitchen was quite an odyssey, in part because my idea of marmalade totally differed from my mother's. She had always followed a recipe from Nanny, her Swiss nursemaid (who, years later, also took care of me). The result was a very sweet, classic British-style marmalade. I wanted my marmalade to taste fresh, bright, and very fruity, as if you were biting straight into a tangerine. This is where I ran into trouble with Giovanna, as well. I hoped to use very little sugar and cook the fruit only a short amount of time. But Giovanna knew that the sugar and the cooking were what gave the marmalade a long shelf life. We finally made a deal—less sugar but a longer cooking time. Fortunately, the marmalade was delicious, so I think this was a good compromise.

That first year, Giovanna and I, plus my two other helpers, Enza and Carmela, worked closely in the kitchen, rhythmically chopping, seeding, grinding, stirring together the sugar and the citrus pulp, and finally letting the concoction rest overnight in giant plastic tubs. The next day, the "line" started over again as we cooked and jarred the mixture. My mother and father even joined us to stick labels on the jars. We were shocked when we realized that we had produced ten thousand jars of marmalade in eight days! At the time, I was still living most of the year in Rome, and I remember opening the door to my apartment and getting funny looks from my daughter, Virginia, who could still smell the tangerine on me.

For my orange marmalade, I mostly use a variety called Tarocco, whose bright orange skin becomes striped with red after the first frost. The garden at Case Vecchie doesn't produce enough fruit for our marmalade needs, so I collect more from my friend Rudolf von Freyberg, whose property is located between Siracusa and Catania. The area's volcanic soil, combined with the Sicilian sun, produces, I think, the best organic Tarocco in Sicily. When making marmalades that use the entire fruit, including the peel, it's important that the fruit be free of any chemical treatment. Because much of the pectin is found in the seeds, I gather the seeds in cheesecloth and boil them with the sugared pulp. Other than that, the only real secret to my jam is that I use the freshest possible citrus: The sooner you prepare the jam after the fruit has been harvested, the better it will be.

Marmellata di Arance
Orange Marmalade

3 pounds oranges, preferably organic

4½ cups sugar, divided

Remove the stem end and any bruises from the oranges, then quarter them. Remove as many seeds as possible and set them aside, covered. Pass the fruit, including the peel, through a meat grinder on the coarsest setting, or shred the fruit in batches in a food processor. Transfer the orange pulp to a large bowl and stir in 2¼ cups sugar. Let the mixture stand at room temperature for about 10 hours, or overnight.

Transfer the sugared pulp to a large saucepan and stir in the remaining 2¼ cups sugar. Wrap the reserved seeds in a square of cheesecloth, tie securely, and add to the saucepan. Bring to a boil, then immediately reduce the heat to low and cook, stirring often so the mixture does not stick to the bottom of the pan, until thickened, 30 to 40 minutes.

To test the marmalade, drop a spoonful on a plate and cool for 1 minute. Tilt the plate: The marmalade should remain in a soft mound. If the marmalade runs, continue cooking, testing often, until done.

Spoon the hot marmalade into sterilized half-pint jars. Seal tightly and turn the jars upside down to cool. Store in a cool, dark place.

Note: To make Marmellata di Mandarino (Tangerine Marmalade), follow the procedure above, but use 3 pounds tangerines and 3½ cups sugar, divided (stir 1¾ cups sugar into the tangerine pulp, then add the remaining 1¾ cups sugar when cooking the mixture).

— Makes about 7 half-pint jars

Of all the many kinds of marmalades we make, lemon is the hardest to get right. We usually use a variety called Femminello Comune, which has an intriguing perfume and a fairly thick peel. Because the thick skin tends to release a great deal of pectin, the marmalade can become a bit too jelled. To make it somewhat softer, I add more juice and omit the seeds. The results are splendid—softly set, with a great balance of sweet and sour notes.

Marmellata di Limone
Lemon Marmalade

3 pounds lemons, preferably organic

5½ cups sugar, divided

Juice about one-third of the lemons and set the juice aside.

Remove the stem end and any bruises from the remaining lemons, then quarter them. Remove as many seeds as possible and discard. Pass the fruit, including the peel, through a meat grinder on the coarsest setting, or shred the fruit in batches in a food processor. Transfer the lemon pulp to a large bowl and stir in the reserved juice and 2¾ cups sugar. Let the mixture stand at room temperature for about 10 hours, or overnight.

Transfer the sugared pulp to a large saucepan and stir in the remaining 2¾ cups sugar. Bring to a boil, then immediately reduce the heat to low and cook, stirring often so the mixture does not stick to the bottom of the pan, until thickened, 30 to 40 minutes.

To test the marmalade, drop a spoonful on a plate and cool for 1 minute. Tilt the plate: The marmalade should remain in a soft mound. If the marmalade runs, continue cooking, testing often, until done.

Spoon the hot marmalade into sterilized half-pint jars. Seal tightly and turn the jars upside down to cool. Store in a cool, dark place.

— Makes about 7 half-pint jars

One year, we made such a huge batch of lemon marmalade that we ran out of jars. So we tried making some sorbet from the leftover sugared pulp—it was one of the most delicious mistakes I've ever tasted, and now I always make my lemon sorbet this way. We tried the same method with tangerine sorbet, but found, strangely enough, that we preferred our original, all-juice formula.

Sorbetto al Limone
Lemon Sorbet

2 cups sugar, divided

1 cup water

2 large lemons, preferably organic, plus ½ cup freshly squeezed lemon juice

Combine ¾ cup sugar and the water in a medium saucepan and cook over medium-low heat, stirring, until the sugar has dissolved and the mixture becomes slightly syrupy. Cool until tepid.

Remove the stem end and any bruises from the lemons, then quarter them. Remove as many seeds as possible and discard. Pass the fruit, including the peel, through a meat grinder on the coarsest setting, or shred the fruit in batches in a food processor. Transfer the lemon pulp to a medium bowl and stir in the lemon juice, cooled sugar syrup, and remaining 1¼ cups sugar. Refrigerate overnight.

Freeze the mixture in an ice cream maker, then transfer to an airtight container and put in the freezer to firm up.

— Makes about 1 quart

Sorbetto al Mandarino
Tangerine Sorbet

3 cups freshly squeezed tangerine juice

¾ cup sugar

Pour the juice through a fine-mesh sieve (to remove any seeds and pulp) into a medium bowl. Add the sugar and stir until dissolved, then refrigerate the mixture until very cold.

Freeze the mixture in an ice cream maker, then transfer to an airtight container and put in the freezer to firm up.

— Makes about 1 quart

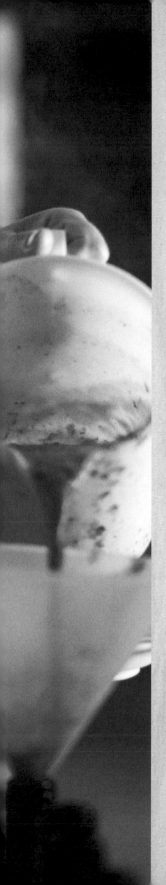

Giovanna is my right arm in the kitchen.

When I am leading a cooking lesson, she follows my moves, ready to step in if I miss something or need help. There is no need for words—she is just always there, discreet and helpful.

Giovanna and her husband, Pompeo, first started working at Case Vecchie in 1994, and they moved into the central house in the courtyard in 2000, when my family hired Pompeo to be the caretaker of the property. They still live there with their teenage children, Antonella and Michele, and when it's cold out, we can just yell to each other from door to door. Giovanna was a real treasure right from the start, and my mother was happy to work with and learn from her, and so am I. Giovanna has the kind of know-how that comes from a lifetime of cooking. From her, I have learned how to be patient when baking or working with pasta dough, how to "read" a dough's texture to know when you have kneaded it enough—the sorts of things you can't learn in a cookbook, only from observing and working beside an expert in the kitchen. I would define it as a sort of breathing transmission of knowledge. Though she can be reluctant to change even a comma of a traditional recipe or something that she learned from my mother, Giovanna has a formidable palate. Like me, she has a sweet tooth, and she doesn't care for acidic flavors, but whenever I want to try a new recipe or experiment, she is right there and knows just how to make it work.

Giovanna was born in Vallelunga and belongs to a family that still makes their own olive oil and tomato paste, so she knows a lot about local cuisine. Both she and her husband have family spread over Europe, and while Pompeo would love to visit them, Giovanna simply shakes her head and won't even consider it. Her aversion to anything from outside Vallelunga has its acme in her feeling about Palermo and its citizens, who are, according to Giovanna, rude and uncivilized, some sort of *cafoni*. This is just to say that she is proudly and consistently local.

Marmalades and sorbets aren't the only way we preserve citrus. At breakfast, I carefully peel my orange and hang the ribbon of rind beside the window. Once it has dried, I use it to make tea or grind it up with dried herbs for our Case Vecchie Herb Blend (page 236). Meanwhile, Giovanna makes huge amounts of candied orange and lemon peel, which we use to decorate cakes or Sfince (page 90), the fried puffs we traditionally make for the feast of San Giuseppe in March.

Scorzette di Arancia
Candied Orange Peel

3 oranges, preferably organic

1 cup sugar

Using a small, sharp knife, cut off a small slice from the top and bottom of each orange to expose the fruit, then score the peel from top to bottom at ⅓-inch intervals, cutting through the pith. Pull off each strip of peel, including the pith, and drop into a large bowl (reserve the fruit for another use). Cover the peels with well-salted water (1 heaping tablespoon salt per 1 quart water) and soak for 24 hours, placing a plate over the peels to keep them submerged.

After 24 hours, rinse the peels repeatedly to remove the salt, then drain well. Place the peels and sugar in a large nonstick pot and add enough water to just cover the peels. Cook over low heat, stirring occasionally, until the sugar melts, then simmer gently until the peels become transparent and the sugar has become syrupy and reduced, about 20 minutes. Remove from heat and, using tongs or a fork, arrange the candied peel on a rack set over wax paper. Cool the peels completely, then transfer them to a glass jar and store in the refrigerator.

— Makes about 50 pieces

One February, chef David Tanis visited me at Case Vecchie. It was the time of year when Sicilian lemons are at their very best—big, pale yellow, and very juicy. For dessert, I used the lemons that grow in our garden in Mondello to prepare my favorite lemon cream. The intense flavor of those lemons took David by surprise, and his reaction made me realize how such a basic ingredient as a lemon—when it is at its peak—can make a huge difference in a meal.

Crema di Limone
Lemon Cream

3 lemons

3 eggs

1¼ cups sugar

6 tablespoons cornstarch

3 cups water

Finely grate the zest of the lemons, then juice the lemons and set aside separately. Combine the eggs, sugar, cornstarch, and zest in a bowl, and beat with an electric mixer on high until well combined and thickened, about 5 minutes.

Transfer the egg mixture to a medium saucepan and stir in the water and reserved lemon juice. Cook over medium heat, stirring constantly, just until the mixture begins to boil, 10 to 15 minutes. Remove from the heat and strain through a fine-mesh sieve into a large shallow serving bowl or individual glasses. Cool before serving. This is delicious served with fresh, ripe berries.

—Serves 6 to 8

I feel I cannot control my sweet tooth unless I experiment with making new desserts for others. One day, I had some lemon cream left over from the night before. To keep myself from inhaling it during that dangerous hour between four and five in the afternoon, I decided to stuff the tangy cream into *cuddureddi*, an airy, raised doughnut. Essentially a brioche dough made with lard instead of butter, this pastry is a slightly richer recipe than Sicilians usually admit to. The delicious result reminded me of early mornings when my uncle took my cousins and me to school and would treat us to warm doughnuts dripping with marmalade. Irresistible!

Cuddureddi
Raised Doughnuts

2½ cups all-purpose flour

2 teaspoons fresh compressed yeast

1¼ cups lukewarm whole milk

1 tablespoon lard

Pinch of fine sea salt

Vegetable oil, for frying

1 cup sugar

1 teaspoon ground cinnamon

2 cups Crema di Limone
(page 19), optional

Mound the flour on a work surface and make a well in the center. Add the yeast, milk, lard, and salt to the well. Gradually stir in enough flour with your hands to form a paste, then work in the remaining flour to form a dough and knead until very smooth (the dough will still be quite sticky). On a floured work surface, roll the dough out to a 1-inch thickness, then cut into rounds with a 3-inch cookie cutter. Cut holes from the middle with a smaller cutter. (If you plan on stuffing the *cuddureddi* with the lemon cream do not cut out a hole from the middle.) Place the cut pieces of dough on a baking sheet lined with parchment paper and let rise for about 30 minutes.

Heat 2 inches of oil in a deep heavy skillet over medium-high heat. Slip a few pieces of dough into the hot oil and fry on one side until golden brown, 1 to 2 minutes, then flip carefully and fry until golden brown, another minute or so. Remove from the oil with a slotted spoon or skimmer and transfer to paper towels to drain. Repeat with the remaining dough.

Mix together the sugar and cinnamon in a bowl, and dredge the *cuddureddi* in the sugar mixture.

If desired, fill a pastry bag with the lemon cream. Insert the tip and squeeze the cream into the *cuddureddi*. Serve at room temperature.

— Serves 8

All over Italy, people make their own limoncello, and why not when it's so simple? I prefer a very clean limoncello; compared to dense commercial liqueurs, ours has a soft, mild taste. We serve it at the close of the meal with our green almond and walnut liqueurs, Mandorlino (page 151) and Nocino (page 151). I also use it in Cassata (page 66), to give a kick to the cake's sweetness.

Limoncello
Lemon Liqueur

4½ cups water

2 cups sugar

6 lemons, preferably organic

1 (750 ml) bottle 95-proof grain alcohol

Combine the water and sugar in a medium saucepan and cook over medium-low heat, stirring, until the sugar has dissolved and the mixture becomes slightly syrupy. Cool until tepid.

Using a vegetable peeler, remove the zest (avoiding the pith) from the lemons and place in a 3-quart jar with a lid (reserve the fruit for another use). Add the alcohol and cooled sugar syrup and mix well. Screw the lid onto the jar and put in a cool, dark place for 2 to 3 weeks.

Pour the limoncello through a fine-mesh sieve into sterilized bottles or jars and seal tightly.

— Makes about 2½ quarts

The citron is a fantastic fruit that is almost unknown outside of Italy and Israel. It looks like an enormous lemon, and underneath its yellow skin is a thick layer of white, spongy pith and a firm, sour heart about the size of a walnut. In Sicily, we call it a cedro lemon. While living in Rome I tried desperately to find cedro lemons, but when I finally did, the taste was somehow somewhere else! Although not bad, those Roman cedros tasted very different from the aromatic, jasmine-flavored ones that we grow at Case Vecchie. Sliced, skin and all, they make a lovely salad with crisp fennel. If you cannot find cedro lemons, use the best-quality regular lemons you can and round out the salad with lettuce.

Insalata di Cedro e Finocchio
Cedro Lemon and Fennel Salad

3 fennel bulbs, cored and very
   thinly sliced, preferably on
   a mandoline

1 pound cedro lemons, very thinly
   sliced, preferably on a mandoline
   (do not remove peel)

¼ cup extra-virgin olive oil

2 tablespoons red or white
   wine vinegar

1 teaspoon dried oregano,
   preferably wild

½ teaspoon fine sea salt

¼ teaspoon black pepper

Mix all the ingredients together in a large bowl. Let stand at room temperature
for 15 minutes before serving.

— Serves 6 to 8

Pompeo, the caretaker at Case Vecchie, introduced me to this recipe, the best orange salad I've ever had. It's very colorful, with the right balance of tang, heat, salt, and acidity. Blood oranges are essential; if you use navel oranges, it turns into a fruit salad, which we don't want! Pompeo's original recipe called for smoked herring, a surprising ingredient for people in the middle of Sicily to use. When I make it these days, I prefer to use anchovies, which I always have on hand, or to replace the fish entirely with thin slices of aged pecorino.

Insalata di Arance, Cipolle Rosse e Olive Nere
Blood Orange Salad with Red Onion and Black Olives

2 large or 4 small blood oranges

1 head escarole, pale inner leaves torn into bite-sized pieces and darker, outer leaves reserved for another use

1 small red onion, halved lengthwise and thinly sliced

12 oil-cured black olives, pitted

4 anchovy fillets, coarsely chopped

¼ cup extra-virgin olive oil

2 tablespoons red or white wine vinegar

½ teaspoon red pepper flakes

Generous pinch of dried oregano, preferably wild

Fine sea salt

With a sharp paring knife, remove the peel and the membranes from the oranges. Working over a large salad bowl, cut the segments free from the membranes, letting them drop into the bowl. Add the escarole, onion, olives, and anchovies to the bowl.

Just before serving, gently toss the salad with the oil, vinegar, red pepper flakes, oregano, and salt to taste.

— Serves 6

THE HOLIDAYS

Mario Lo Menzo, my grandparents' longtime chef, was a sweet, fat man with beautiful pale hands and a long rectangular face framed by lots of dark hair neatly combed backward from his large forehead. Even after hours of working in the kitchen, he was always cool and calm. Looking at him, you would never guess that he came from a very poor family. He was born in a small town called Mistretta, on the northwest coast of Sicily, and arrived at my grandparents' house when he was just sixteen, joining the kitchen staff as a dishwasher and helper to chef Giovannino Messina. Over the years, he rose through the ranks and became chef himself.

Mario once told me that he learned to cook so well by "stealing" Giovannino's secrets with his eyes, not an easy task since the chef would invent an excuse to get Mario out of the kitchen any time he had a complicated recipe to work on. Once he took over the kitchen, Mario, of course, did exactly the same thing with his pupils. Whenever my mother would ask him about the measurements for a recipe, he would smile and nod, answering with a vague "As much as you need" or "It depends." At his worst, he would gesture impatiently with his hands, which meant, "I never bother with measurements!"

Mario's specialty was a sort of Franco-Sicilian cooking, the so-called *monsù* cuisine (a corruption of the word "monsieur"). It is a complicated and delicious blend of ancient Sicilian recipes—with all of their many Greek, Roman, and Moorish influences—and French style, which had become fashionable with Europe's aristocratic families at the end of the eighteenth century. *Monsù* cuisine introduced lots of buttery sauces, eggy dishes, creamy béchamel, and meat sauces to the more vegetable- and grain-based Sicilian diet.

A perfect example of Mario's cooking was his rich brioche filled with béchamel and ham, which he made for the Prince of Wales when he visited my grandparents at Regaleali. Mario's recipe called for 14 egg yolks plus 2 whole eggs—quantities I couldn't even fathom when my grandmother asked me to take over making the brioche after Mario retired. I knew I was on dangerous ground, because I was making the brioche for the world's toughest critics—my family—and I just couldn't bring myself to use so many eggs. My friend Anna Maria Dominici, an eighty-year-old cook who occasionally offers cooking classes at her house in Palermo, taught me how to make it lighter, by using 1 egg for every scant cup of flour.

With brioche dough, the softer and stickier it is, the better. I started working with the dough the day before so that it could rest overnight before I rolled it out and stuffed it. Happily, the dough came together, and when I gently turned it upside down, the huge, fluffy top stayed strong and didn't crack! Now I have made it many, many times, and no one misses all those extra eggs. I do have one other little secret: I like to fold some orange zest into the dough; it rounds out the flavor of the brioche and helps temper its richness.

A few tips: To create a strong seal, always fold the side edges in and then place the top round of dough over it, rather than the other way around. Also, wait at least 20 minutes before unmolding it, so that the béchamel can cool slightly and collect itself; otherwise you run the risk of the heavy filling breaking the crust and ruining all of your hard work!

Brioche Ripiena
Stuffed Brioche

DOUGH

3¼ cups all-purpose flour

¾ cup bread flour

4 teaspoons fine sea salt

1 teaspoon fresh compressed yeast

⅔ cup lukewarm whole milk, divided

3 eggs

¼ cup sugar

9 tablespoons cold butter, cut into small pieces

1 teaspoon finely grated orange zest

FILLING

4 tablespoons butter

6 tablespoons all-purpose flour

2 cups whole milk

Pinch of nutmeg

Fine sea salt and black pepper

4 ounces prosciutto cotto (boiled ham), cut into small pieces

4 ounces Gruyère, cut into small pieces

4 ounces Italian Fontina, cut into small pieces

4 ounces finely grated Parmesan

¾ cup frozen peas, blanched

1 egg, lightly beaten, for egg wash

Make the dough: Mix the two flours and salt together in a bowl. Mound the flour mixture on a work surface and make a well in the center. Dissolve the yeast in about half of the lukewarm milk. Add the yeast mixture, 2 of the eggs, the sugar, butter, and orange zest to the well. Gradually stir in enough flour with your hands to form a paste, then knead the remaining flour into the mixture with your hands to form a soft dough. Knead the dough on a lightly floured work surface until it pulls away from your hand easily. Then add the final egg and the remaining milk and knead again until the dough is smooth and elastic (it will still be quite sticky). Place the dough in a large bowl and set aside, covered with a towel, to let rise for 30 minutes. Then immediately transfer the dough to the refrigerator to slow the rising and let rest overnight. (This will make the dough easier to work with the next day.)

The next day, make the filling: Melt the butter in a medium saucepan, then remove from the heat and whisk in the flour. Gradually whisk in the milk, then return the pan to medium heat and cook, stirring constantly, until the béchamel sauce has thickened, about 10 minutes. Season with the nutmeg and salt and pepper to taste. Set the béchamel aside to cool.

Preheat the oven to 350°F. Butter a 10-inch springform pan and lightly dust with flour.

Divide the dough into two pieces, one slightly larger than the other. Roll out the larger piece of dough on a lightly floured surface into a 16-inch round, about ⅓ inch thick. Fit into the pan, letting the excess dough hang over the sides. Roll out the smaller piece of dough into an 11-inch round and set aside.

Cover the bottom of the dough with the ham (this will help "seal in" the liquid). Then stir together the béchamel, cheeses, and peas, season with salt and pepper, and spread over the ham. Fold the excess dough onto the top of the filling. Brush the top of these folds with the egg wash, then "seal" everything with the reserved round of dough. Brush the top of the dough with some egg wash (reserve the remainder of the beaten egg for the next step). Put the prepared brioche near your preheated oven and allow to rise until the dough has risen significantly, 30 minutes to 1 hour.

Brush the top of the dough with some more of the egg wash and bake until the top of the brioche is golden brown and the bread is cooked through, about 45 minutes. Cool on a rack for at least 20 minutes before loosening the sides of the pan. Either serve on the pan bottom, or carefully transfer to a serving dish.

— *Serves 12*

Though we ate Mario's *monsù* cooking year-round with my grandparents, its extravagance peaked at Christmas time. When my grandparents were still alive, the whole family celebrated the holidays at Regaleali or Villa Tasca. Our extended family is so large that we can only all get together once or twice a year, and not surprisingly, Christmas dinner has always been huge and very special. Even today, now that we usually celebrate in Mondello, the Christmas table is not complete without a big dish of pasta, platters of chicken galantine and headcheese, a huge fish such as salmon or dentice seasoned with home-made mayonnaise, chicken liver pâté with truffles, and a giant stuffed turkey. Accompanied by several little dishes like green olive salad and fried appetizers such as *ghineffi* or *uova alla monacale*, the meal is a real triumph. For dessert, there are tangerine baskets filled with tangerine gelatin and profiteroles with chocolate sauce, plus all sorts of traditional Sicilian sweets that friends and family bring from little *pasticcerie* tucked away in some small village or hidden in Palermo's side streets.

I remember eating *uova alla monacale* very often at cocktail hour at my grandparents' house when I was a child. The idea is to hard-boil eggs, remove the yolks, and then refill the whites with a rich mixture made of the mashed yolks, béchamel, and grated Parmesan. The eggs are then battered and fried—quite impressive!

Uova alla Monacale
Fried Stuffed Eggs

4 tablespoons butter

⅓ cup plus ½ cup all-purpose flour, divided

2 cups whole milk

2 tablespoons finely grated Parmesan

Pinch of nutmeg

Fine sea salt and black pepper

6 hard-boiled eggs, cooled, peeled, and halved lengthwise

1 cup water

2 uncooked eggs

3 cups unseasoned dried breadcrumbs

Vegetable oil, for frying

Generously butter a baking sheet or plate; set aside.

Melt the butter in a medium saucepan, then remove from the heat and whisk in ⅓ cup flour. Gradually whisk in the milk, then return the pan to the heat and cook, stirring constantly, until very thick, about 10 minutes. Stir in the Parmesan, nutmeg, and salt and pepper to taste.

Carefully remove the yolks from the hard-boiled eggs and mash with a fork until smooth. Add the yolks to the béchamel and stir until well combined. Fill each egg half with a heaping spoonful of the béchamel mixture and lay facedown on the buttered baking sheet or plate, so the béchamel can cool and compact.

Meanwhile, whisk together the remaining ½ cup flour, the water, and the uncooked eggs in a large shallow dish until smooth and creamy. Fill another large shallow dish with the breadcrumbs.

When the béchamel-stuffed eggs are cool, gently loosen with a spatula and dip them in the batter, then dredge in the breadcrumbs. Heat 2 inches of vegetable oil in a large heavy skillet over medium-high heat. Add the battered eggs in batches and fry until golden, 1 to 2 minutes per side. Remove from the oil with a slotted spoon or skimmer and transfer to paper towels to drain. Sprinkle with salt and serve hot.

Note: I like to make small croquettes with any leftover béchamel filling. To do so, turn the chilled béchamel out onto a floured work surface and roll it into olive-size pieces. Dip first in the batter, then in the breadcrumbs, and fry. These croquettes are especially tasty with a bit of grated Gruyère or chopped ham folded into the béchamel.

— Makes 12

The south of Italy, and Sicily especially, has a long tradition of deep-frying foods. Guests are sometimes shocked by how much we fry at the cooking school, but they are even more surprised by how light and crisp our *panelle*, *arancine*, *pizzelle*, and other fried dishes taste; they are never heavy or greasy. As I like to say, a well-fried homemade *arancina* is less harmful for you than any kind of commercial mass-produced snack.

Because Sicilian home cooks do so much frying, they are very comfortable with the process and never bother to fiddle with thermometers. It's simply a matter of practice. A few tips: Don't be afraid of using lots of oil when you are deep-frying; the food really needs to float in the hot oil to cook properly. Don't be timid about getting the oil properly hot; this is what helps keep the greasiness at bay. The shock of entering the hot oil seals the outside of the food and keeps the oil from seeping in. I check to see if the oil is ready by sticking the handle of a wooden spoon in the oil; when the oil immediately starts bubbling around the handle, I know I am ready to start. It's also very important to stay at the stove when you are frying; that way you can adjust the temperature as needed. Turn it up a little when you slip the food in (cold food entering the hot oil will bring the temperature down), or turn it down if you see it starting to smoke or if things are browning too quickly. Sometimes I even turn the heat off completely for a minute or so while I'm frying and then turn it back on as needed. Finally, guests often assume that I fry everything in olive oil, but I actually use vegetable oil most of the time. I find it much more forgiving than olive oil, which can start smoking very quickly. Plus, vegetable oil has a much more neutral, clean taste, which lets the flavor of whatever you are frying shine through.

Ghineffi were one of my passions as a kid, and they still are today. We like to eat these tiny fried risotto balls as an appetizer paired with an iced white wine or as a first course in beef or chicken stock. The *ghineffi* should be rolled no larger than one-half inch, and they can drive you mad if you don't have enough patience!

Ghineffi
Fried Risotto Balls

2 tablespoons extra-virgin olive oil

1 cup arborio rice

2 cups chicken stock

½ cup finely grated Parmesan

2 tablespoons butter

½ cup all-purpose flour

1 cup water

2 eggs

3 cups unseasoned dried breadcrumbs

Vegetable oil, for frying

Fine sea salt

Combine the oil and rice in a medium saucepan and "toast" the rice over medium heat until a slight change in color occurs, 1 to 2 minutes. Add the chicken stock and as soon as it comes to a boil, cover and remove from the heat. Let stand, covered, until the stock is fully absorbed, about 20 minutes (it should be fairly stiff). Stir in the Parmesan and butter, then spread out onto a large buttered plate to cool.

Meanwhile, whisk together the flour, water, and eggs in a shallow bowl until smooth and creamy. Fill another shallow bowl with the breadcrumbs. Roll the cooled risotto into ½-inch balls. Working in batches, dip the balls into the batter, then into the breadcrumbs and set aside on a clean baking sheet.

Heat 2 inches of oil in a large heavy skillet. Add the risotto balls in batches and fry until pale golden, about 1 minute. Remove with a slotted spoon or skimmer and transfer to paper towels to drain. Sprinkle with salt and serve hot.

Note: To serve in soup, prepare the chicken broth from Capellini in Brodo con Ricotta (page 55) and ladle into bowls. Pass the ghineffi *on a separate dish so everyone can add as much as they want.*

— Makes 40 to 50

Neither my mother nor I could ever reproduce Mario's chicken liver mousse, so eventually I had to search for my own. My friend Isabella Ducrot, an artist who was born in Naples and now lives in Rome, shared this recipe with me. I like to make a big batch of this mousse and freeze it in little cups so I can pull one out to serve as an appetizer any time somebody drops in for dinner. With a good loaf of rustic bread, it is really delicious.

Mousse di Fegatini di Pollo
Chicken Liver Mousse

¼ cup extra-virgin olive oil

1 small red onion, chopped

1 garlic clove, peeled

2 pounds chicken livers, cleaned

½ teaspoon fine sea salt

¼ teaspoon black pepper

1 cup white wine

½ cup fresh sage leaves

1 small bunch fresh thyme

1 large sprig fresh rosemary

1 orange, halved

1 lemon, halved

¼ cup Grand Marnier or other orange-flavored liqueur

1½ sticks (6 ounces) butter, cut into pieces

Combine the olive oil, onion, and garlic in a large heavy skillet and cook over medium heat until the onion is softened, about 5 minutes. Increase the heat to medium-high, add the chicken livers, salt, and pepper, and cook until the livers are lightly browned, about 5 minutes. Add the wine, herbs, orange, and lemon and reduce the heat to medium. Partially cover and continue to cook until the liquid has evaporated by at least half, 10 to 12 minutes. Uncover and continue to cook until the liquid has all but evaporated, then add the Grand Marnier and cook until the alcohol has evaporated. Remove from the heat and cool for 5 minutes. Discard the orange, lemon, and herbs (don't worry if you don't get every piece).

Transfer the chicken liver mixture to a food processor and puree until combined. Add the butter and continue to puree until very smooth. If desired, pass through a sieve for a more refined texture. Serve at room temperature or slightly chilled.

— Serves 8 as a first course, 12 to 14 as an hors d'oeuvre

The recipes I inherited from Mario are precious to me because they are part of a history of Sicilian aristocratic cuisine that has yet to be fully written and express an attitude toward ingredients that hardly exists anymore. In dishes like chicken galantine, you can see the practice of transforming an ingredient by changing its appearance but keeping, and exulting in, its taste. Translated into contemporary terms, maybe such an attitude can be found in molecular gastronomy?

A year before he died, Mario allowed me to film him while he prepared a galantine. He was suffering from diabetes and confined to a wheelchair, but he was happy to show me how to debone a chicken, then stuff, roll, and tie it. Despite his trembling hands and exhaustion, his galantine was, as always, perfect.

Galantine might appear intimidating but in fact all you need is time and a good butcher to debone the chicken if you don't know how to do it yourself. This is a delightful main course for a buffet.

Galantina di Pollo
Chicken Galantine

1 (4-pound) chicken, deboned and butterflied

6 ounces prosciutto cotto (boiled ham), chopped

¾ cup shelled pistachios, coarsely chopped

1 teaspoon fine sea salt

½ teaspoon black pepper

Place the chicken on a cutting board breast-side down and open it into a sort of square shape. In order to make a more even surface, shave off the parts of the breast and thigh that stick up higher than the rest of the meat. Chop the shaved-off meat with the ham in a food processor until finely chopped. Transfer to a bowl and stir in the pistachios, salt, and pepper.

Spread the meat and pistachio mixture evenly over the chicken, leaving a ½-inch border all around. Beginning with the edge closest to you, roll up tightly. Once the entire chicken is rolled up, wrap well with foil, twisting the ends tightly. With butcher's string, tie the galantine as you would a roast. Place the galantine in a pot large enough to hold it, cover with water, and bring to a boil. Reduce to a simmer and cook for 1 hour, then remove from the water and cool. Refrigerate. When ready to serve, thinly slice and serve cold.

— *Serves 12*

Strange to say, but one of our most beloved family traditions comes from the United States, via Gloria Ducrot, one of my grandparents' best friends. Gloria was born in Colombia, raised in New York, and met her future husband, Enrico Ducrot, in 1926 on the maiden voyage of the *Roma*, whose itinerary was Nice–Napoli–New York. The Ducrot family owned one of the most fashionable furniture factories in the 1920s and had furnished the ocean liner. Gloria and Enrico married in 1931 and moved to Palermo, where they and my grandparents became friends. After Gloria gave her this recipe, my grandmother started to raise turkeys at Regaleali. She always had six or so turkeys at a time because the local fox seemed to appreciate them so, and she wanted to make sure there would still be one around for Christmas dinner. Since the family has been celebrating Christmas in Mondello, I have taken over making this giant turkey stuffed with sausage, chestnuts, and breadcrumbs.

Tacchino Ripieno
Stuffed Turkey

1 (16-pound) fresh turkey

12 bay leaves, preferably fresh, divided

Zest of 2 lemons

½ cup extra-virgin olive oil

1 large onion, chopped

1 carrot, peeled

1 celery stalk

4 sprigs fresh flat-leaf parsley

2 pounds sweet Italian sausage (preferably a blend of pork and veal), casings discarded

4 garlic cloves, finely chopped

Fine sea salt and black pepper

1 cup white or red wine

4 eggs

1 (14.8-ounce) jar cooked whole chestnuts, coarsely chopped (alternatively, boil about 1½ pounds fresh chestnuts, then peel and chop)

8 cups unseasoned dried breadcrumbs

4 ounces ground pistachios

2 tablespoons Case Vecchie Herb Blend (page 236)

Put the turkey in a very large stockpot or bucket with 10 bay leaves and the lemon zest. Cover with cold water and refrigerate for 24 hours.

The next day, combine the olive oil and onion in a large skillet and cook over medium heat until softened, about 5 minutes. Meanwhile, with butcher's string, tie together the carrot, celery, parsley, and remaining 2 bay leaves to make a bouquet garni. Add the sausage, garlic, bouquet garni, and salt and pepper to taste to the onion and cook, stirring occasionally, until the sausage is browned and cooked through, 10 to 15 minutes. Add the wine and cook, uncovered, until mostly evaporated, about 5 minutes. Remove from the heat and cool.

Beat the eggs in a small bowl until well combined. When the sausage mixture is cool, gently stir in the beaten eggs, chestnuts, breadcrumbs, and pistachios. Set aside.

Preheat the oven to 375°F. Remove the turkey from the soaking liquid, drain well, and pat dry. Place in a large roasting pan. Rub the skin all over with the herb blend, salt, and pepper. Loosely stuff the turkey cavity with the sausage mixture (stuffing will expand as it cooks; if there is any remaining, transfer to a buttered baking dish and bake separately), and truss to keep the stuffing from falling out. Roast the turkey until a meat thermometer inserted into the thickest part of the thigh registers 175°F (stuffing should register 160°F), 3 to 4 hours.

Remove the stuffing and transfer to a dish. Cover the turkey loosely with foil and let turkey stand for 20 minutes before carving. Serve with pan juices.

— Serves 12 to 16

My father, Venceslao Lanza, is probably the best-looking man I've ever known, but what's even more striking, he is a man of words. He joined my mother at the cooking school during the last ten years or so that she was active; before then, I would say that my mother's kingdom was not available to him. When he did enter, an interesting "play" started between the two of them for the guests. While she was the pioneer rediscovering local peasant cooking, he played the part of the fussy aristocrat brought up on the art of French cuisine, disdaining tomato sauce and wild greens (he belongs to one of Sicily's oldest families and proudly states that the Lanzas came over with Frederick II in the thirteenth century). But in fact, they both loved the simple act of eating!

My father is a marvelous conversationalist. He belongs to that lost breed of people who were brought up knowing all the secrets of entertaining: Never let the conversation falter; always stay alert and survey your partner's interest and curiosity; and be able to express a wide knowledge of history, art, and politics without showing off. Watching guests become enchanted by his stories always fills me with pride, and I do love when he joins me at Case Vecchie.

Fresh tangerine skins filled with tangerine-flavored gelatin are a refreshing way to end a big meal. Mario always added tangerine essence to his gelatin. When my mother started the cooking school and introduced this recipe, she made the jelly with tangerine juice only—no essence was allowed—and served it in glasses rather than the tangerine skins. This set off a mini revolt in the family, since some preferred her way and others were loyal to Mario's version. As for me, I feel that the skins impart a very special fragrance to the gelatin, so now I do make the baskets but omit the tangerine essence from the gelatin.

Panierini di Gelatina di Mandarino
Tangerine Baskets Filled with Tangerine Jelly

20 tangerines, divided   2 cups sugar

6 gelatin sheets

Select the 8 prettiest tangerines, and set aside the remainder for juicing. Working with one tangerine at a time and being careful not to cut the fruit inside, cut through the peel around the top of the tangerine, roughly ½ to 1 inch from the stem. Carefully remove the top, making sure to keep the top and the rest of the tangerine intact. Reaching through the center of the fruit, gently remove one segment of tangerine after another, until all the fruit is gone and you are left with a "basket" (reserve the fruit for another use). Arrange the baskets in a baking dish or on a small baking sheet, then set aside while you make the gelatin.

Juice enough of the remaining tangerines to measure 4 cups juice. Pour the tangerine juice through a fine-mesh sieve into a bowl to remove any seeds and pulp. Place the gelatin sheets in a small pan of cold water to soften. Combine 2 cups tangerine juice with the sugar in a medium saucepan and cook over low heat, stirring, until the sugar is dissolved. Add the gelatin, one sheet at a time, and stir until fully melted. Remove from the heat and stir in the remaining 2 cups tangerine juice. Refrigerate the mixture until beginning to set, 1 to 2 hours, then spoon it into the tangerine baskets and put the tops back in place. Refrigerate until set, about 6 hours.

Note: Tangerine baskets can also be filled with Tangerine Sorbet (page 13) and frozen.

— Serves 8

Until I left Palermo at eighteen, every Christmas and birthday party included Mario's profiteroles. Once my children were born, I wanted to make the profiteroles myself for their birthdays. I had no recipe, and Mario was his usual vague self, but I had my palate and knew exactly how they should taste. After much trial and error, my profiteroles now taste just like the ones I had in my childhood.

Profiteroles con Cioccolato e Panna
Profiteroles with Chocolate and Whipped Cream

PÂTE À CHOUX

½ cup water

4 tablespoons butter

Pinch of fine sea salt

⅔ cup all-purpose flour

2 eggs

CHOCOLATE SAUCE

1¼ cups sugar

1¾ cups good-quality unsweetened cocoa powder

⅔ cup cornstarch or wheat starch

4 cups whole milk

FILLING

1 cup heavy cream

1½ teaspoons sugar

Make the pâte à choux: Combine the water, butter, and salt in a medium saucepan and bring to a boil. Add the flour all at once and stir rapidly until the dough pulls away from the sides of the pan. Transfer the dough to a bowl to cool completely, then add the eggs, one at a time, mixing thoroughly after each.

Preheat the oven 400°F. Fit a pastry bag with a large tip and fill the bag with dough. Pipe dough onto a parchment-lined baking sheet in 1-inch-high mounds, about 1½ inches apart. Bake until the puffs have doubled in size and are golden, about 20 minutes. Transfer to a rack and cool.

Make the chocolate sauce: Whisk together the sugar, cocoa, and cornstarch in a large saucepan, then whisk in the milk and cook over medium heat, whisking often, until the sauce is smooth and thickened, about 20 minutes.

Make the filling and assemble: Whisk the cream and sugar together until soft peaks form. Fill the puffs with the cream and drizzle with the chocolate sauce.

— Serves 8

Compared to profiteroles, the *buccellati* Giovanna and I make every Christmas are the other side of the moon! Whereas profiteroles are light and airy and all about contrasting flavors and textures, these sturdy fig-filled cookies are about finding the right balance. None of the filling ingredients—dried figs, walnuts, pistachios, almonds, tangerine marmalade, and vino cotto—should overwhelm another. Americans are surprised by the use of ammonium bicarbonate, but it is often used as a leavener in Sicily (we also use it in Taralli, page 210). It dries up the humidity in the dough during baking and gives the cookies their unique crispness.

Buccellati
Filled Fig Cookies

FILLING

6 ounces dried figs

½ cup finely chopped walnuts

2 tablespoons finely chopped pistachios

2 tablespoons finely chopped almonds

½ cup Tangerine Marmalade (page 8) or good-quality store-bought marmalade

½ cup vino cotto

DOUGH

4 cups all-purpose flour

½ cup sugar

½ cup plus 2 tablespoons lard

2 eggs

½ teaspoon vanilla extract

1 tablespoon powdered ammonium bicarbonate, also called hartshorn

Milk, as needed

ICING

1 cup powdered sugar

Juice of 1 lemon

Colored sprinkles, for decorating

Make the filling: Put the figs into the bowl of a food processor and pulse until ground to a thick paste. Transfer the figs to a medium saucepan with the walnuts, pistachios, almonds, tangerine marmalade, and vino cotto. Cook over low heat, stirring frequently, until the figs soften and the mixture thickens, about 15 minutes. Remove from the heat and let cool.

Preheat the oven to 350°F.

Make the dough: Mound the flour in a large bowl and make a well in the center. Add the sugar, lard, eggs, vanilla, and ammonium bicarbonate to the well and gently mix with your hands. Add the flour to the ingredients in the center little by little, until a dough forms. If the dough is too dry, add some milk, drop by drop, until it comes together. You should be able to knead and roll it on a work surface without it sticking.

Take a quarter of the dough and roll it into a long rectangle, about 3 inches wide and ¼ inch thick. Fill a pastry bag with the cooled filling and pipe the filling (about ½ inch wide) along the bottom third of the dough (alternatively, you can use a small spoon to spread the filling). Carefully fold the bottom of the dough over the filling and then fold the top over, so that the filling is enclosed within the dough. Turn the log seam-side down and press gently to flatten. With a sharp knife, cut the log into 3-inch lengths. Gently bend each cookie into a crescent shape, then cut 2 or 3 slits along the rounded edge of the dough. Transfer the cookies to two unlined baking sheets, and repeat with the remaining dough and filling.

Bake until the cookies are light golden brown, about 25 minutes. Transfer the cookies to a rack to cool completely.

Meanwhile, make the icing: Stir together the sugar and lemon juice in a small bowl until smooth. When the cookies are cool, brush with the icing and decorate with the colored sprinkles.

— Makes 4 to 5 dozen cookies

When I see my young nephews, nieces, cousins, and their friends scream-ing with excitement on New Year's Eve as fireworks explode over the fields of Regaleali, memories of my own childhood come rushing forward. I can feel the freeze on my ears and nose as I tucked in close to my cousin Filiberto, while we waited along the enormous stone wall of Case Grandi for the same fireworks ritual. "Along the wall" was the rule and not a step forward, otherwise it was straight to bed without getting to share my grandmother's midnight banquet, when everyone would gather around the huge dining room table and eat together.

Other than a few must-have dishes, such as a platter of lentils ("Because they bring money!") and an exquisite lamb dish that Mario made with Regaleali's Rosso del Conte, the New Year's Eve meal had no specific tradition— anything good could land on the table. Because Mario's lamb requires a full day to marinate, I now make my own lamb stew with mint, which I serve with saffron stewed potatoes.

Spezzatino di Agnello alla Menta
Stewed Lamb with Fresh Mint

½ cup extra-virgin olive oil

1 large red onion, chopped

3½ pounds boneless lamb shoulder
  or leg, cut into 2-inch cubes

1 tablespoon *estratto* or good-
  quality sun-dried tomato paste

1 cup red or white wine

Pinch of saffron

8 cups water

Leaves from 1 large bunch fresh
  mint, chopped

Fine sea salt and black pepper

Combine the olive oil and onion in a large, deep saucepan and cook over medium-high heat until just golden, about 5 minutes. Add the lamb and stir until well coated in oil. Stir the *estratto* into the wine until dissolved, then add to the pan and cook until evaporated, about 2 minutes. Combine the saffron and water, then pour over the lamb to cover. Cover and bring to a boil. Reduce to a simmer and cook, covered, about 40 minutes. Prop the lid open with a wooden spoon and continue to simmer until the lamb is tender, about 20 minutes more. If the sauce is too liquidy, uncover completely to let evaporate (the sauce should be thickened and somewhat creamy). Stir in the mint and season to taste with salt and pepper.

— Serves 10

Patate allo Zafferano
Saffron Stewed Potatoes

¼ cup extra-virgin olive oil

1 large red onion, finely chopped

4 pounds russet (baking) potatoes, peeled and cut into big chunks

Pinch of saffron

4 cups water

Fine sea salt and black pepper

Pinch of dried oregano, preferably wild

Combine the olive oil and onion in a large pan and cook over medium heat until softened, about 5 minutes. Add the potatoes and stir until well coated in oil, about 5 minutes. Combine the saffron and water, then cover the potatoes with the saffron water (add more water if necessary to just cover). Add a pinch of salt, then bring to a boil over medium-high heat, covered, and cook for about 40 minutes, checking often and stirring to make sure the water does not evaporate too quickly. When the potatoes are done, they should be creamy on the outside but still a bit firm inside. Stir in the oregano, plus salt and pepper to taste.

— Serves 10

COMFORT FOOD

As you can see, when my grandparents were still alive and Mario was cooking for them, meals at Regaleali were abundant and rich, quite intense from a digestive point of view. But as soon as my mother and I were alone, we liked to share light, tasty soups made with greens freshly harvested from the vegetable garden. It was such a treat to sit across from my mother at the blue kitchen table in Mondello, talking quietly and sipping the "dirty water," as my father called it, with kale or escarole floating together with broken bits of spaghetti and strands of melted cheese.

Minestra di Scarola e Provola
Escarole Soup with Provolone

¼ cup extra-virgin olive oil

1 small red onion, finely chopped

1 head escarole (about 1½ pounds), chopped into 2-inch pieces

Fine sea salt

6 cups warm water

1 cup small dried pasta, such as ditalini, or spaghetti that has been broken into 1-inch pieces

4 ounces diced young provolone, *primo sale*, or *tuma*, diced

Combine the olive oil and onion in a large saucepan and cook over medium heat until softened, about 5 minutes. Add the escarole and cook for another minute, turning it to coat with the oil. Add 1 teaspoon salt and cover with the warm water. Bring to a boil, then reduce to a simmer, cover, and cook until escarole is tender and silky, about 20 minutes. Season with salt if needed. If the soup is too thin, uncover and cook until slightly reduced.

Meanwhile, cook the pasta in a medium pot of boiling well-salted water. Drain and add to the soup. Divide the cheese among soup bowls, then ladle the soup over the cheese.

— *Serves 4*

Mimma, the housekeeper at the winery, used to make a kale and potato soup for my uncle when he returned from hunting trips on the property. When I tasted her delicious soup, I understood the true purpose of the amazing kale that grows in the Madonie Mountains, especially near the town of Caltavuturo, and that Carmelo, one of our gardeners, has now planted in our vegetable garden. The huge leaves are very dark green and crisp, and their taste is sweet and rich. Because the soup is so basic, it is probably one of the trickiest recipes I've ever made. You need to get the proportions just right, otherwise you risk the dreaded "dirty water."

Minestra di Cavolo e Patate
Kale and Potato Soup with Fresh Mint and Parsley

10 cups water

1½ pounds kale, preferably lacinato, chopped into 2-inch pieces

1½ teaspoons fine sea salt

3 medium russet (baking) potatoes, peeled and cut into 1-inch pieces

1 garlic clove, peeled and smashed

½ cup finely chopped fresh mint leaves

½ cup finely chopped fresh flat-leaf parsley leaves

¼ cup extra-virgin olive oil

Bring the water to a boil in a large pot. Add the kale and salt and cook over medium-high heat, uncovered, for 15 minutes. Add the potatoes and cook until very tender, about 25 minutes. Remove from heat and stir in the garlic, mint, parsley, and oil. Cover and let stand for 5 minutes for the flavors to meld. If desired, discard the garlic clove before serving.

— Serves 4 to 6

The most comforting food of all is capellini cooked in broth and served with fresh ricotta; this is a soup both my mother and my grandmother ate with immense pleasure up until their last days. When David Gould, a lovely young chef who now cooks at the Brooklyn restaurant Roman's, spent a few weeks at the cooking school, I often made this soup for him and my parents. I assume David loved it too, since the dish appeared on the menu when the restaurant opened!

Capellini in Brodo con Ricotta
Capellini in Chicken Broth with Ricotta

2 pounds chicken parts

¼ pound veal stew meat

1 carrot, peeled and cut into chunks

1 celery stalk, cut into chunks

1 medium onion, coarsely chopped

4 sprigs fresh flat-leaf parsley

5 quarts water

Fine sea salt

1 pound capellini

6 tablespoons ricotta, preferably sheep's milk

Parmesan, for serving

To make the broth, combine the chicken, veal, carrot, celery, onion, parsley, and water in a large pot. Bring to a boil, then reduce the heat and simmer, skimming froth occasionally, until broth is golden and richly flavored, about 3 hours. Remove from the heat, discard the chicken, veal, and vegetables, cool, and refrigerate.

When ready to make the dish, skim fat from the top of the broth and pour through a fine-mesh sieve into a clean pot. Bring the broth to a boil. Season with salt, add the capellini, and cook until al dente. Divide the pasta and broth among soup bowls, stir a spoonful of ricotta into each bowl, and top with grated Parmesan.

— Serves 6

SHEEP'S MILK CHEESES

During childhood visits to Regaleali, I always checked on the sheep first. I would leap out of the car, my eyes scanning the hills dotted with gnarled olive trees until I spotted their woolly shapes. In the autumn, the lambs were left in the paddock while their mothers went out to graze on the first green grasses growing after the harsh summer heat. This was the moment I could catch hold of a lamb and take it in my arms. Its scrambling attempts to escape always scared me, but I held on long enough to embrace its soft, bony body and inhale the sweet fragrance of its mother's milk. When the ewes came back, our shepherd, Totuccio, started milking them. I could never bear the taste of this warm milk—it was too strong and sheepy tasting—but I loved watching him make cheese.

The best cheese at Regaleali is made during the winter because that is when the hills around the estate are simply carpeted with wild greens, aromatic and fresh. The sheep wander the hills with their shepherd for most of the day, sating themselves on the fragrant green bounty and only coming home to sleep and to be milked. Because there is such a variety of herbs and greens growing on the mountains of Sicily, each valley produces a different tasting pecorino, *primo sale*, and ricotta. If we spoke of cheese like wine, I would say that our ricotta is one of the foods that best expresses the personality of our terroir.

At Regaleali, the cheesemaking process has changed very little over the years. Once Totò, our current shepherd, has collected the milk, he takes it to the dairy, an old stone building lined with blue tile, and sets to work. Everything in the room has a purpose, and nothing is wasted, not even the shepherd's gestures. The milk is cooked in an enormous pot over a wood-burning fire, but it must not boil; it should just reach the right temperature so that the rennet will melt and the milk will curdle and rise to the surface. Some Sicilian shepherds use a plant-based rennet, such as the milky sap from a fig leaf, but Totò still prepares a very traditional rennet from the stomach lining of a young lamb, one that has eaten only its mother's milk. It takes about an hour for the milk to start coagulating, and Totò stirs the warm milk with a long stick to break up the coagulated surface into pea-size curds. He then spoons the curds into large baskets, pressing down on them to compress the cheese until it is solid. This "first" cheese is called *tuma*. It can be eaten immediately—raw, it has a delightful squeak to it—or baked until bubbly with herbs and vinegar in the dish known as Formaggio all'Argentiera. I like to eat this with bread and salad for a casual vegetarian supper.

Formaggio all'Argentiera
Baked Cheese with Vinegar and Oregano

¼ cup extra-virgin olive oil, divided

1 pound *tuma*, provolone, or any good melting cheese (but not too drippy like mozzarella), cut into ½-inch-thick slices

2 tablespoons red wine vinegar

Large pinch of dried oregano, preferably wild

Preheat the oven to 375°F. Drizzle a large ceramic baking dish with half the olive oil, then arrange the sliced cheese snugly in the dish and drizzle with remaining olive oil. Bake until the cheese begins to melt. Once the edges of the cheese begin to brown, drizzle the vinegar over the cheese and sprinkle with the oregano. Turn off the oven, then return the cheese to the still-warm oven and let stand for 5 to 10 minutes more. Serve immediately.

— Serves 4 to 6

Tuma is the base for *primo sale* ("first salt") and then for pecorino. To make these cheeses, Totò cuts the *tuma* into blocks and presses them into perforated plastic baskets. At one time, the cheesemaking baskets were made of straw, but now almost everyone has switched over to plastic. A little of the romance has been lost with the use of this modern convenience, but at least the plastic baskets are modeled after the original woven straw ones, so the final cheese bears the same pattern. Sometimes he folds black peppercorns or coriander seeds into the *tuma*, two traditional flavorings here. To become *primo sale*, the *tuma* sits for a couple of hours in the leftover brine, then Totò coats it with salt once and puts it to rest on a wooden shelf. Over the next few days, he gently rubs the cheese with any juices that are released through the basket. After a week the *primo sale* is done and can be eaten. A longer wait in the leftover brine and at least three months on the shelf lead to pecorino.

To produce ricotta, a little more milk is added to the whey that is left over from making the *tuma*, and the mixture is gently heated. As the creamy concoction comes up to the surface, Totò gently collects it with a spoon and puts it into more small baskets to drain. Regaleali's ricotta is a dream, like eating a cloud. When it is fresh and still warm, I eat it in the morning for breakfast, with fresh fruit or honey; but once the ricotta has aged a couple of days, it becomes a superb ingredient for filling cassata, cannoli, *cassatelle*, and ravioli.

When my grandparents still lived at their villa in Palermo, a small lorry would deliver the warm, juicy ricotta from Regaleali to the city. My grandmother then distributed it to her children: her son, Lucio, and her three daughters, Anna (my mother), Costanza, and Rosemarie. And although my grandparents are no longer alive, our driver, Loreto, still makes deliveries to our family in Palermo every Tuesday. What a happy sight it is to see his truck loaded down with fresh *tuma*, ricotta, and *primo sale*!

I consider cassata the *summa* of all Sicilian culinary adventures and history. I imagine this magnificent cake's trail leading from the ancient Romans (*cassata* probably comes from the Latin *caseus*, for cheese), to the Moors, who may have provided the candied fruit and the frame of marzipan, and finally to the Spanish, who were known for their superb colorful decorations. I learned how to make cassata from my mother, who was especially proud of her version and liked to repeat her friend Mary Taylor Simeti's compliment that after she had tried my mother's cassata she could never eat any other.

Cassata
Sponge Cake with Ricotta Cream and Marzipan

SPONGE CAKE

6 eggs, at room temperature

¾ cup sugar

1 teaspoon finely grated orange or lemon zest

1⅓ cups flour, sifted

RICOTTA CREAM

2 cups whole-milk ricotta, preferably sheep's milk

½ cup sugar, or to taste

MARZIPAN

1¾ cups almond flour

½ cup shelled pistachios, very finely ground

¾ cup powdered sugar

1 to 2 tablespoons water

½ teaspoon liquid glucose or light corn syrup

Green food coloring

ASSEMBLY

¼ cup Limoncello (page 22) or Grand Marnier, divided

2 cups powdered sugar

Juice of 1 to 2 lemons

Candied fruit, for garnish

Make the sponge cake: Preheat the oven to 350°F. Butter and flour a 10-inch springform pan. With an electric mixer, beat the eggs until pale, about 5 minutes. Add the sugar and zest and continue to beat until the mixture has thickened and ribbons form when the beaters are raised, about 15 minutes. Gently fold in the flour. Pour the batter into the prepared pan and bake until a knife inserted into the center of the cake comes out clean, 25 to 30 minutes. Transfer the pan to a rack to cool completely.

Make the ricotta cream: Stir together the ricotta and sugar until light and fluffy. Set aside.

Make the marzipan: Mix together the almond flour, ground pistachios, and powdered sugar, and mound together on a work surface. Make a well in the center and add 1 tablespoon water, the glucose, and a few drops of green food coloring to the well. Knead the mixture together like a dough so that everything is evenly incorporated (if the mixture is too dry, add more water, drop by drop). Dust a work surface with powdered sugar, then roll out the marzipan ¼ inch thick. Cut the marzipan into long, 2-inch-wide strips. Knead the remaining marzipan into a ball, wrap it in plastic wrap, and store in the refrigerator for later use.

To asssemble, line a 12-inch cassata pan, or a 12-inch pie pan, with plastic wrap. Line the sides of the pan with the marzipan strips, pressing together at the seams to make one continuous band. Trim any excess.

Cut the cake crosswise into ½-inch-thick slices. Line the bottom of the pan with a layer of cake slices, trimming to fit. Drizzle 2 tablespoons limoncello over the cake. Spread the ricotta cream evenly over the cake slices. Carefully top the ricotta cream with another layer of cake slices, trimming to fit (you may not use all of the cake slices). Drizzle with the remaining 2 tablespoons limoncello.

Make the icing: Whisk together the powdered sugar and enough lemon juice to form a smooth, shiny icing with a thin spreading consistency.

Invert the cassata onto a large serving plate. Carefully lift off the pan and peel off the plastic wrap. Pour the icing over the top of the cassata and smooth with a spatula, leaving the marzipan sides of the cake visible. Decorate the top of the cake with candied fruit. Refrigerate the cake until set, about 2 hours.

— Serves 10 to 12

Cassatelle are a new mainstay at Case Vecchie, thanks solely to my terrible sweet tooth. These fried pastries stuffed with sweetened ricotta are the "croissants" of western Sicily; any café in the Trapani area makes them, and people have them with coffee in the morning or as a dessert.

Cassatelle
Ricotta-Filled Turnovers

7 tablespoons white wine

3 tablespoons extra-virgin olive oil

2 cups semolina flour

Pinch of fine sea salt

1 cup whole-milk ricotta,
   preferably sheep's milk

3 tablespoons granulated sugar

½ teaspoon ground cinnamon,
   plus more for garnish

Vegetable oil, for frying

Powdered sugar, for garnish

Combine the wine and oil in a small saucepan and heat until just warm (not hot). Mound the flour on a work surface and make a well in the center. Add the wine-oil mixture and salt to the well, and with a fork, carefully incorporate it into the flour. Knead the dough with your hands until smooth and elastic. In a separate small bowl, stir together the ricotta, granulated sugar, and cinnamon, and set aside.

Set a pasta machine to the widest setting. Run a piece of dough through the machine about 5 times at this setting, folding the dough in half each time before rolling it again. When the dough is very even, move the dial to the next setting and roll it through 2 to 3 times more, folding it each time. Move the dial to the third setting and roll it through 2 or 3 more times. Lay out the dough on a floured work surface, and cut out circles with a 4-inch round cookie cutter. Place a spoonful of ricotta just off-center, then moisten the edges of the dough with water and fold over. Pinch to seal. Repeat with remaining dough and filling.

Heat 2 inches of oil in a large, heavy skillet. Add the *cassatelle* in batches and fry, flipping occasionally, until deep golden, about 3 minutes. With a slotted spoon or skimmer, transfer to paper towels to drain. Sprinkle with powdered sugar and cinnamon. Serve warm.

— Makes about 18

I don't think that you can find better *cannoli* in all of Sicily than the ones we make at Regaleali. The lightness of the freshly made ricotta cream and the crispness of the shells are quite amazing! At one point, a sort of competition emerged between my mother at Case Vecchie and Maria, the chef at Case Grandi after Mario's death, and they proudly tested their cannoli against each other. It was a narrow competition, but in the end, there was no doubt that Maria's cannoli were slightly better than my mother's, whose shells often popped open during frying. The amount of flour Maria used, whether or not she added butter to her dough, how much vinegar or wine (or both!) she added—these were all secrets that were fiercely hidden in the little streets of Vallelunga, where Maria has lived all her life.

But the odds tipped in our favor one day when I was wandering alone through Palermo's Ballarò neighborhood, where a lively melting pot of Arab, Sri Lankan, and Nigerian market stalls are set up next to Palermitan street vendors, and everything from fresh spleen and the long pale zucchini known as *cucuzze* to papayas, mangos, and yuca is for sale. While meandering through the narrow streets of this vibrant place, I discovered a dark, almost windowless *laboratorio* where the extensive Rosciglione family produces thousands of cannoli shells a day, at a rhythm that astounded me. I couldn't believe I'd never heard of this shop or that such a family enterprise still existed. I soon learned that the Roscigliones are one of the largest Palermitan families devoted to traditional pastry. One brother split off and opened a store on the other side of the city that sells all sorts of Sicilian pastries, while Mimmo and his huge family stuck to cannoli shells, which they sell throughout Italy.

At this little artisanal industry, one huge electric mixer was used to prepare the dough, then the dough was rolled out into long velvety ribbons by a pasta machine, but the rest was all done by hand. The sheets of dough were cut into rounds, then the individual rounds were dusted with flour, piled on top of one another, rolled around cylindrical wooden molds, and fried in huge fryers. The shells that bobbed up from the oil were excellent: crunchy and not too sweet, with just the right thickness. The three Rosciglione brothers, as well as the daughters and sons working there, were very generous, since they gave me a rough recipe. (No pastry chef in Sicily will ever give you the exact recipe, and I can understand why—it took them so long to achieve perfection!) Now the cannoli at Case Vecchie don't open when we fry them, and they are as tender and crisp as ever. I dare say, if there were another cannoli competition, we would win!

Cannoli con Crema di Ricotta
Cannoli with Ricotta Cream

CANNOLI SHELLS

2 cups all-purpose flour

4 teaspoons lard

2 teaspoons sugar

2 teaspoons unsweetened
  cocoa powder

Pinch of fine sea salt

¼ cup vinegar or wine,
  or as needed

1 egg, lightly beaten,
  for egg wash

Vegetable oil, for frying

RICOTTA CREAM

1½ cups whole-milk ricotta,
  preferably sheep's milk

½ cup sugar, or to taste

Candied Orange Peel (page 18),
  for garnish

Make the cannoli shells: Combine the flour, lard, sugar, cocoa, and salt in a bowl and mix together with your hands. Add the vinegar, bit by bit, and knead until the dough comes together. (The dough should be quite stiff.) Set a pasta machine to the widest setting. Take a piece of dough and run it through the machine 7 to 10 times at that setting, folding the dough in half each time before rolling it again. When the dough is very even, continue to roll it through the machine, once at each setting without folding, until you reach the next to last setting (the dough should be very even and silky). Lay the dough out onto a lightly floured work surface and with a lightly floured 4-inch cookie cutter, cut out rounds. Wrap the dough rounds around metal or wooden cannoli molds, dab the edge with egg, and press to seal. Repeat with the remaining dough, rerolling the scraps.

Heat 2 inches of oil in a wide, heavy pot over medium-high heat. Add the cannoli shells in batches and fry until the shells have become bubbly, crisp, and browned, 4 to 5 minutes. With tongs, transfer to paper towels to drain. Cool and remove the molds carefully.

Make the ricotta cream: Beat together the ricotta and sugar until smooth and creamy. With a small spoon, fill the cannoli shells, then decorate with the candied orange peel.

— Makes about 20

Seasoned with herbs and spices, our ricotta makes a wonderful stuffing for savory dishes. I use it for my favorite ravioli recipe, which I discovered during one of my trips to Pantelleria, a large island between Sicily and the north coast of Africa, where I have gone since I was a child. It is a feast dish for the island, one that they now sell in pasta shops because people don't have as much time these days to prepare it at home. Because Pantelleria is a volcanic island with extremely rich soil, powerful sunshine, and little rain, ingredients grown there have very intense flavors. To replicate those flavors in my ravioli, I use a strong Sicilian peppermint that I grow in the courtyard of Case Vecchie. I also like to stir in a nice pinch of nutmeg and cinnamon to the filling. Served with tomato sauce, as below, the ravioli are sweet and comforting; they are equally good, but very different, topped with Almond and Sage Pesto (page 153).

Ravioli di Ricotta e Menta
Ravioli Stuffed with Ricotta and Mint

PASTA DOUGH

2 cups all-purpose flour

2 cups durum wheat or semolina flour

4 eggs

Pinch of fine sea salt

FILLING

1½ cups whole-milk ricotta, preferably sheep's milk

2 tablespoons finely grated Parmesan

½ cup fresh mint leaves, finely chopped

Pinch of ground nutmeg

Pinch of ground cinnamon

Pinch of ground hot pepper

ACCOMPANIMENT

4 cups Salsa Pronta (page 163) or good-quality tomato sauce, warmed

Ricotta Infornata (page 79), finely grated

Make the pasta dough: Combine the flours, mound on a work surface, and make a well in the center. Add the eggs and salt to the well, and with a fork, carefully start working the flour in until a shaggy dough forms. Knead the dough until smooth and elastic, 8 to 10 minutes.

Make the filling and roll out the pasta: Stir together the ricotta, Parmesan, mint, nutmeg, cinnamon, and hot pepper in a medium bowl. Set a pasta machine to the widest setting. Take a piece of dough and run it through the machine several times at that setting, folding the dough in half each time before rolling it again. When the dough is very even, continue to roll it through the machine, once at each setting without folding, until you reach the last setting. Lay the pasta sheet horizontally on a lightly floured work surface. Place spoonfuls of ricotta filling a few inches apart near the top edge of the dough and fold the pasta in half to enclose it. Cut the dough into rounds or squares and press to seal. Repeat with the remaining dough and filling.

Cook the ravioli in boiling well-salted water until they rise to the surface and are tender, about 6 minutes. Arrange on a large serving platter and top with the warmed tomato sauce and finely grated *ricotta infornata*.

— Serves 6

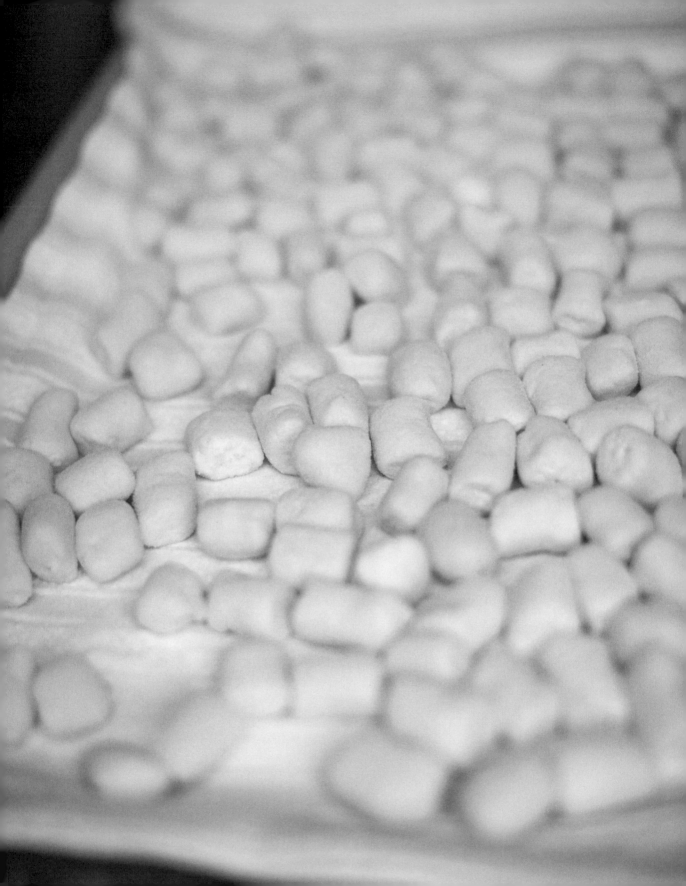

My Uncle Gioacchino's wife, who is from Venice, always complains that we don't have the right potatoes in Sicily to make gnocchi. And she's right—there is no potato culture in Sicily. If you go to the market, the most you will find are two varieties, basically called "old" and "new" potatoes. So at Case Vecchie we like to prepare gnocchi with ricotta. The secret to light, tasty dumplings, as I always tell guests, is finding the right balance between the flour and ricotta. You need flour to hold the dough together, but you must use as little as possible so that the flavor of the ricotta, and not the flour, dominates.

Gnocchi di Ricotta
Ricotta Gnocchi

1 pound whole-milk ricotta, preferably sheep's milk

1 egg

3 tablespoons all-purpose flour, or as needed

2 tablespoons finely grated Parmesan, plus more for serving

Semolina flour, for dusting

4 cups Salsa Pronta (page 163) or good-quality tomato sauce, warmed, or 1½ sticks melted butter and chopped sage

Gently combine the ricotta, egg, all-purpose flour, and Parmesan in a bowl. If the mixture is too soft to come together like a sticky dough, add a little extra flour (the dough should be moist and fairly sticky).

Dust a work surface with semolina flour, then take a small piece of dough and very gently roll it into a ¾-inch-thick rope. Cut the rope into ¾-inch pieces and transfer to a towel that is lightly dusted with semolina flour. Repeat with the remaining dough.

Once all the gnocchi are prepared, bring a large pot of well-salted water to a boil. Carefully gather up the ends of the towel so that you can gently drop all the gnocchi into the pot at once. Boil the gnocchi until they float to the surface, about 2 minutes.

Serve with the tomato sauce or butter and sage leaves and grated Parmesan.

— Serves 6

Until a few decades ago, Parmesan was practically nonexistent in Sicilian cuisine. Instead, Sicilians served their pasta dishes with grated pecorino or *ricotta infornata*—ricotta that has been drained and then baked at a very low temperature until it is hard enough to grate. These days, Parmesan is available everywhere, and the use of baked ricotta is not so common anymore. We still make some in the winter when we bake bread in the wood-burning oven or more simply in the convection oven. Once the ricotta is baked, we slice it and freeze it so that it can last longer. Together with wild oregano and homemade *estratto*, *ricotta infornata* is something I always bring with me when I travel—these are the ingredients that give me a taste of home.

We usually bake sheep's milk ricotta, since that is what is mostly produced in our area. But a bit higher in the Madonie Mountains, you will find a few men and women who keep cows and make cow's milk ricotta. Unfortunately, since the European Union laws are now very strict, these people and practices are disappearing. It is far too expensive to convert a simple hut with a wooden fire into a sterile room with a gas stove and steel and tile surfaces. One day I was lucky enough to meet Giuseppina, who hides up in the mountains away from EU inspectors and produces a lovely salted ricotta with cow's milk.

Salting the ricotta has the same purpose as baking it does, but the results are quite different. The baked ricotta is still a bit soft, with a gently smoked flavor. It still tastes intensely like ricotta. The salted ricotta has a much more even texture and obviously the ricotta flavor is somewhat hidden by the salt. This is where Giuseppina really works her magic: She knows just the right amount of salt to use so that it dries the ricotta without obscuring its flavor and turning it into, as we would say, *un pezzo di sale*—a piece of salt.

Both kinds of cheese are meant to be grated on pasta, and they melt and blend with the noodles and sauce in a very different way from Parmesan or grated pecorino, adding a pleasing touch of creaminess.

Ricotta Infornata
Baked Ricotta

4 pounds whole-milk ricotta,
  preferably sheep's milk

2 to 3 tablespoons fine sea salt

Special equipment: a 2- to 3-quart
  clay pot

Place the ricotta in a large fine-mesh sieve and set over a bowl. Cover with a towel and drain, refrigerated, until most of its liquid has been released, 3 to 5 days (empty the liquid from the bowl periodically and discard).

Preheat the oven to 225°F. Pat the drained ricotta into the shape of the clay pot, then lightly coat each side of the ricotta with the salt. Pack the ricotta firmly into the pot and bake, uncovered, until the top and sides are deep brown, 10 to 12 hours. Cool in the pot overnight, then remove the ricotta from the pot and dry at room temperature until it reaches a grating consistency, about 24 hours. Cut into wedges, wrap well, and store in the freezer.

— Makes about 2 pounds

PREZZEMOLO
26/11
POMODORO GROSSO
26/11
SEDANO
26/11
SEDANO
26/11
L. 4 STAGIONI
26/11
L. 4 STAGIONI
26/11

SPRING

Spring in Sicily is truly the stuff of legends: The Lake of Pergusa lies near the town of Enna, just a few miles from Regaleali, and it was there that Hades kidnapped the beautiful Persephone to the underworld. In retaliation, her mother Demeter, the goddess of the harvest, plunged the land into drought. When Hades finally relented and returned the girl to her mother for six months of the year, Demeter smiled again on Sicily, restoring the balance of the seasons.

This is the moment when spring comes out in all its rainbow glory, and the land is covered with a tangle of sweet peas, wild roses, bright red poppies and tulips, yellow dyer's broom, purple French honeysuckle, stalks of wild fennel, and the spiky pink and yellow blooms of cardoons.

At Case Vecchie, we know spring is on its way when the almond tree near the entrance to the property becomes covered with a cloud of little white blossoms. The almond fruits are far from ready—we will harvest them in June and then again in August when they have dried in the sun—but the airy flowers tell us that winter's freeze is over. As the soil warms up, the garden comes back to life, and soon we are feasting on a steady stream of artichokes, wild fennel, fava beans, and lentils.

THE FEAST OF SAN GIUSEPPE

For centuries, the feast day of San Giuseppe, March 19, has marked the beginning of spring in Sicily. It's an important day for Sicilians, of whom at least one out of three seems to be named for the saint. My interest in this feast day started quite casually. I was visiting some friends who told me about women in remote parts of Sicily building incredible altars and filling them with food as a sign of gratitude to San Giuseppe that a family member had recovered from some danger or illness. The women would start cooking a week before the feast day, preparing a huge amount of specific, ritualistic dishes. The food would then be offered to the three poorest children of the village, who represented the holy family.

I had to see this tradition for myself. I borrowed the most basic video camera I could find and went to the village of Ramacca, not far from Caltagirone. Ramacca is, I think, the ugliest town I have ever seen. It is utterly without charm—no stone walls, no old acacias, no shady squares with oleander trees. I could not imagine the extraordinary beauty I would find behind those mean, concrete facades. In fact, what I saw totally changed my perspective on food and on the significance it can have in Sicily.

When I walked into Concetta's house, I saw that all the beauty, skill, and fantasy missing from the village's streets were on display on her altar honoring San Giuseppe: golden breads in elaborate shapes, colorful cookies, ripe fruits, and all sorts of fried vegetables. The three children invited to celebrate the ritual meal looked as stunned as I did, though I'm sure they also felt even more self-conscious since my camera was staring at them. But then came the first course: Concetta had prepared for each child a small glass of *biancomangiare*. I was amazed to see this sweet almond pudding offered as a first course, but I was told that it was to break the fast and prepare the three guests for what was to come. Concetta then served *macco*, a lovely soup of fava beans, followed by an innumerable variety of fried foods—cauliflower, artichoke, cardoon, and wild fennel fritters—before they finished with the fried puffs known as *sfince di San Giuseppe*, which the kids seemed to enjoy the most. We all clapped when a new dish was served, and Concetta said a prayer of thanks to the saint for his mercy and generosity while the kids ate their meal. When the children had finished and all the leftovers were given to their families, Concetta's family and I finally sat down at the table and ate the same meal. I think the *macco* was the best I have ever tasted in my life.

Biancomangiare
Almond Pudding

4 cups whole milk

⅔ cup cornstarch or wheat starch

¾ cup sugar

2 teaspoons almond extract

Ground cinnamon, for garnish

Finely chopped pistachios, for garnish

Whisk together the milk, cornstarch, sugar, and almond extract in a medium saucepan. Cook over medium heat, whisking constantly to prevent sticking, until thickened and creamy (the custard should have the consistency of béchamel), 20 to 25 minutes. Remove from the heat and divide the custard among small glasses. Garnish with a dusting of cinnamon and a sprinkling of pistachios. Cool.

— Serves 6 to 8

Macco
Fava Bean Soup

⅔ cup extra-virgin olive oil, divided

1 medium red onion, finely chopped

3 pounds (about 6 cups) shelled fresh or frozen fava beans, blanched and peeled

4 cups hot water

1 cup wild fennel, blanched and chopped (optional)

Fine sea salt and black pepper

1 cup ditalini or other small dried pasta (optional)

Combine ⅓ cup olive oil and the onion in a wide pot and cook over medium heat until softened, about 5 minutes. Add the fava beans and stir to coat with the oil, then add the water, wild fennel (if using), and a pinch of salt. Bring to a boil, then reduce the heat and cook, partially covered, until the fava beans break down to form a puree, about 30 minutes.

Stir in the remaining ⅓ cup olive oil and season with salt and black pepper to taste.

Meanwhile, cook the pasta (if using) in a small pot of boiling well-salted water. Divide the soup among bowls and top with the pasta. Serve immediately.

— Serves 6

Sfince di San Giuseppe
Fried Puffs with Honey

1 cup water

5 tablespoons unsalted butter, cut into pieces

Fine sea salt

½ teaspoon baking soda

2 cups all-purpose flour

6 eggs, at room temperature

Vegetable oil, for frying

1 cup honey, warmed

24 pieces Candied Orange Peel (page 18), for garnish

Combine the water, butter, and a pinch of salt in a saucepan and cook over medium heat until the butter melts and the water boils rapidly. Add the baking soda (the mixture will bubble up), then add the flour and stir vigorously until well combined and the mixture pulls away from the sides of the pan. Remove from the heat and cool.

When the mixture has cooled completely, transfer it to the bowl of an electric mixer and beat the eggs in one at a time, beating until very smooth.

Heat 2 inches of oil in a large heavy skillet. Spoon out almond-size pieces of dough and carefully push them off the spoon with your fingers into the hot oil. Fry several at a time, but do not crowd the skillet; the puffs need room to turn as they swell (the puffs will triple in size). Cook, turning with a skimmer or tongs, until golden brown on all sides, about 3 minutes. Drain on paper towels. Fry the remaining puffs in batches, letting the oil get hot again before starting each new batch. With tongs, dip the puffs in the warmed honey and garnish with a piece of candied orange peel.

— Makes about 24

WILD FENNEL

The feast of San Giuseppe could also be considered a celebration of wild fennel, since it is around this time that everyone collects the plant and stores it for the rest of the year. It grows everywhere in Sicily and is at its best between mid-February and the end of March. I was happily surprised when I discovered huge, five-foot-tall wild fennel plants growing along the highways of California. I have often wondered if the original seeds were imported by Sicilian immigrants who could not do without it!

The wild fennel in Sicily rarely reaches such a height because we continuously harvest it when it is still small and tender. The best part of it, as Salvatore, one of the caretakers at Case Vecchie, proudly shows me when we are on a wild fennel campaign, is the tender white stock and the little green heart found in the middle of the plant. That white tender stem is in some ways the equivalent of the round white bulb of domestic fennel, but it is incomparable in terms of taste, which is rounder, deep, and sweetish, with a profound note of pure anise. We also use parts of the hairy green, which has the same tasty note but a different texture, while the green of the farmed fennel has very little taste at all. No substitution is possible, so I always recommend planting seeds and growing your own wild fennel. It needs very little water and does well in both cold and warm temperatures.

According to Salvatore, you must head far from the streets to find the tastiest, most tender wild fennel. He climbs the hills on his old Vespa, and when he returns a few hours later, the scooter is loaded down with bags stuffed full of wild fennel. After collecting the fennel, there is a huge amount of work in separating and discarding the external leaves and saving only the most tender ones. Then it is boiled, packed in small plastic bags, and frozen, to be used throughout the year. I've always been struck by the amount of time that lies behind the preparation of most of our food, but the harvest, the cleaning, and the perserving of fruits and vegetables is never considered time-consuming in a negative way. On the contrary, these practices are almost considered a rite, while also offering a time to think, to chat with one another, and to simply be.

In the spring, we collect all the wild fennel we can,
so that we'll have enough to use throughout the year. We blanch it and freeze it
in small plastic bags, so we can just pull one out as needed and add it to soup or
pasta sauce. This is how we prepare wild fennel before using it in any recipe and
for freezer storage: Remove the tough outer fronds of the wild fennel and discard. Chop about ½ inch off the tops of the fennel and discard. Cook the fennel
in a large pot of boiling salted water until tender, 20 to 30 minutes. Drain well
and cool completely. If desired, chop the fennel into 1-inch pieces before packing
it in resealable plastic bags and freeze.

I have always been very fond of wild fennel, but I took a long sabbatical from eating it after an incident when I was living in Verona. I had to prepare a meal for forty people, and while I was cooking *pasta con le sarde*, one of Sicily's most famous dishes, I was overwhelmed by nausea. The smell of wild fennel is incredibly strong, and the whole house was filled with its scent. Soon after the dinner party, I realized that I was pregnant with Ruggero, but it was years before I could bear the smell of wild fennel. I only resumed eating *pasta con le sarde* after I returned to Sicily.

Now, I try to spend every San Giuseppe in Sclafani, where Totò, my beloved babysitter, still lives. Sardines are hard to get up in the mountains, so they playfully call their fishless dish *pasta con le sarde a mare*, which means, *pasta con le sarde with the sardines out to sea*! In Sclafani, the entire village gathers for the feast meal in a great stone-walled hall that was once a convent. Many of the women of the village volunteer to cook and serve this big meal, which includes all the traditional dishes, plus the pasta with the sardines out to sea.

Pasta con le Sarde
Pasta with Sardines

SAUCE

1 pound wild fennel, washed and trimmed

¼ cup extra-virgin olive oil

1 red onion, finely chopped

1 garlic clove, peeled and smashed

3 cups Salsa Pronta (page 163) or good-quality tomato sauce

1 pound very fresh sardines, scaled, cleaned, boned, tails and heads removed (if desired, reserve 8 to 10 sardines and dip in durum wheat or semolina flour and fry, for garnish)

½ cup pine nuts

½ cup dried currants

1 tablespoon *estratto* or sun-dried tomato paste

½ cup white wine

Fine sea salt and black pepper

BREADCRUMBS

1¾ cups unseasoned dried breadcrumbs

¼ cup extra-virgin olive oil

2 tablespoons sugar

1 garlic clove, peeled and smashed

Pinch of ground hot pepper

Fine sea salt

PASTA

1¾ pounds bucatini or perciatelli

Make the sauce: Cook the wild fennel in a large pot of boiling salted water until tender, 20 to 30 minutes. Drain well in a colander and cool, then finely chop and set aside.

Combine the olive oil, onion, and garlic in a large saucepan and cook over medium-high heat until the onion is softened, about 5 minutes. Add the tomato sauce, sardines, pine nuts, currants, and blanched wild fennel. Stir the *estratto* into the wine until dissolved and add to the sauce. Season with salt and pepper and simmer for about 10 minutes (the sardines will break up while cooking).

Make the breadcrumb topping: Combine the breadcrumbs, olive oil, sugar, garlic, hot pepper, and salt to taste in a small skillet and cook over medium heat, stirring constantly, until the breadcrumbs are golden brown and crunchy, about 3 minutes. Remove from the heat and transfer to a small serving bowl. Remove garlic clove, if desired.

Make the pasta: Cook the pasta in a large pot of boiling well-salted water. Reserve 1 cup of the cooking water, then drain well and mix the pasta thoroughly with the sauce, stirring in some of the pasta cooking water if the sauce looks too dry.

Transfer the pasta to a serving platter, garnish with the fried sardines (if using) and serve with the seasoned breadcrumbs on the side.

Note: To make pasta con le sarde a mare, *simply omit the sardines.*

— *Serves 8 to 10*

The feast of San Giuseppe always falls during Lent, so no red meat is ever allowed on the altars. Instead, great attention is lavished on fried foods, mostly salt cod and various spring vegetables. One of my favorite fritters is wild fennel *polpettine*, popular all over Sicily. The principal ingredient is always wild fennel; what varies is the batter. Giovanna sometimes dips the fennel in a very intense mixture made of semolina, yeast, and spring onions. Those *polpettine* are delicious but a bit heavy for my taste, so we have come up with a simple combination of wild fennel, egg, and Parmesan. We usually serve it as an antipasto before sitting at the table.

Polpettine di Finocchietto Selvatico
Wild Fennel Fritters

1 pound wild fennel, washed
  and trimmed

3 eggs

2 tablespoons finely grated Parmesan

Fine sea salt and black pepper

Vegetable oil, for frying

Cook the fennel in a large pot of boiling salted water until tender, 20 to 30 minutes. Drain very well and cool, then finely chop. Combine the chopped fennel with the eggs, Parmesan, and salt and pepper to taste.

Heat 1 inch of oil in a large heavy skillet. Drop large spoonfuls of fennel mixture into the hot oil and fry until golden, about 1 minute per side. Drain on paper towels. Sprinkle with salt and serve warm.

— Makes about 12

It is interesting to note that each village has its own way of preparing wild fennel. One of the most intriguing is this refreshing salad from Vallelunga, which I think expresses the plant's quintessential anise flavor. Olive oil and good red wine vinegar (please, no balsamic!) marry magnificently with the fennel's particular sweetness.

Insalata de Finocchietto Selvatico
Wild Fennel Salad

¾ pound wild fennel, washed
  and trimmed

¼ cup extra-virgin olive oil

1 tablespoon red wine vinegar

Fine sea salt and black pepper

Cook the fennel in a large pot of boiling salted water until tender, 20 to 30 minutes. Drain well and cool, then coarsely chop and transfer to a salad bowl. Add the olive oil, vinegar, and salt and pepper to taste and toss to combine. Serve chilled or at room temperature.

— Serves 4

I have always been very fond

of wine vinegar, but many years ago I found it almost impossible to find good wine vinegar in stores. Some friends were making their own vinegar, which inspired me to try it myself. So, when one day I noticed a little "mushroom" floating at the bottom of a bottle of Cirio vinegar that had been forgotten on the shelf, I knew it was the right moment. I extracted the gelatinous blob, which we call the mother, from the bottle of vinegar and placed it in a large jar that I filled with red wine and some herbs. Somebody had told me that adding a few pieces of dried pasta, honey, or some fresh fruit would help activate the vinegar's bacteria and accelerate the process, so in that went, too. I let my concoction sit, and after a month or so, the wine had turned into vinegar—and it was delicious! This was twenty years ago and that little jar of vinegar, which was only meant for my family, followed me through all my life changes—Rome, Verona, Feltre, Rome again, before eventually making its way to Palermo and Case Vecchie. Now I have a big barrel in the kitchen at Case Vecchie, and every six months I bottle the vinegar to use throughout the year. To round out the flavor of my vinegar, I have taken to adding some reduced must, or vino cotto, to it as it sits (about twenty percent of the whole amount). Over the years, the mother has grown to an enormous size—it looks like a beautiful beef liver!—and I expect to get many more years of delicious vinegar from it.

Caltavuturo, another village perched in the Madonie Mountains with a splendid culinary tradition, is home to an interesting side dish of wild fennel sautéed with tomato sauce and breadcrumbs. It is very simple, but so tasty and satisfying.

Finocchietto Saltato con Salsa di Pomodoro e Pangrattato
Sautéed Wild Fennel with Tomatoes and Breadcrumbs

1 pound wild fennel, washed and trimmed

¼ cup extra-virgin olive oil

1 small red onion, chopped

1 garlic clove, peeled

1 cup Salsa Pronta (page 163) or good-quality tomato sauce

¼ cup unseasoned dried breadcrumbs

Cook the fennel in a large pot of boiling salted water until tender, 20 to 30 minutes. Drain well, cool, and coarsely chop.

Combine the olive oil, onion, and garlic in a medium skillet and cook over medium-high heat until the onion and garlic are softened, about 5 minutes. Add the fennel and cook 1 minute more, tossing to coat with oil. Add the tomato sauce and cook until heated through, about 1 minute. Stir in the breadcrumbs and cook 1 minute more. Serve immediately.

— Serves 4

ARTICHOKES

Giovanni, Case Vecchie's gardener, and I have had a number of gentle arguments over artichokes. I would love to fill the garden with all kinds of artichokes and cardoons, which can grow to immense heights and sprout huge, furry gray leaves and little prickly artichoke flowers on the top. I'm even tempted by the wild artichokes that only produce a very tiny fruit. I like them simply because they are beautiful and in summer produce a spectacular violet-blue flower. But, as Giovanni points out, they would "steal" space from edible vegetables in the garden. So I make do with our regular Sicilian artichokes, which are still quite different from any I have seen elsewhere in the world. Violet-tinged and tipped by menacing thorns, they are smaller and narrower than the round globe artichokes commonly found in the U.S. We grow and eat them all spring, until the last ones are harvested sometime in June.

My first memories of Easter at Regaleali are of the chocolate-egg hunts my grandmother used to organize and of roasted artichokes. The egg hunt was held either in Case Grandi's courtyard, under the shade of the magnolia tree, or in the vegetable garden, to the great despair of the gardener. A large gang of us kids ran all over, shouting and looking for colored eggs hidden under geranium pots or inside heads of lettuce. But even better were the artichokes, which were roasted on an old box spring set over a fire in the middle of the courtyard. I can still hear the crackle as the artichokes were nestled among the embers, taste the ashes on the outer leaves of the artichokes before arriving at the delicious heart, and feel the oil dripping all the way from my chin to my elbow!

Now it is my turn to host Easter in Case Vecchie's courtyard. My children hide the chocolate eggs for the younger ones, and a crowd of friends and family come to share a feast of anelletti with tomato sauce and ricotta, herb-rubbed lamb ribs, roasted artichokes, of course, and a huge cassata. The artichokes are roasted in the coals of the grill while the lamb ribs and coils of sausage cook above.

When she prepares the artichokes for Easter, Giovanna carefully spreads the thorny leaves with her fingers to reveal the heart, which she drowns with *conzo*, a savory mixture of olive oil, garlic, and mint. It's important to really dig in to the center because once the artichoke is cooked, most of the leaves are burnt and the best part to eat remains the heart, where all the *conzo* has dripped.

Carciofi Arrosto
Roasted Artichokes

2 cups extra-virgin olive oil

Leaves from 1 large bunch fresh
  mint, chopped

3 garlic cloves, finely chopped

Fine sea salt and black pepper

12 medium artichokes

Prepare and light a charcoal or hardwood grill.

In a pitcher or large measuring cup with a spout, whisk together the olive oil, mint, garlic, and salt and pepper to taste.

Trim the stems from the artichokes (so that they can stand upright in the ashes), then carefully spread the leaves apart with your thumbs. Pour some of the mint-garlic oil between the leaves of each artichoke and into the heart, reserving some of the oil for roasting.

When the coals of the grill have burned down, set the artichokes directly in the ashes and turn them every once in a while so that they cook evenly, adding more mint-garlic oil as they roast. The artichokes are ready when they are completely charred outside and tender when gently squeezed, about 1 hour. To eat, discard the charred outer leaves to reveal the tender center.

— Serves 6

I find that almost any kind of wine tastes slightly off after I eat artichokes. But these two recipes are so simple and well balanced that I can happily sip a glass of white wine with them. The fried artichokes are crunchy and tasty, like little potato chips but much lighter. The breadcrumb-stuffed artichokes make a delicious side dish to the Stewed Lamb with Fresh Mint (page 50).

Carciofi Fritti
Fried Artichokes

Juice of 1 lemon

4 medium artichokes

Vegetable oil, for frying

1½ cups durum wheat or semolina flour

Fine sea salt

Add the lemon juice to a medium bowl filled with cold water. Trim and discard the tough outer leaves of the artichokes, then scoop out the fuzzy choke with a sharp spoon and discard. Cut the hearts into ¼-inch slices, dropping them into the lemon water.

Heat 1½ inches of oil in large heavy skillet. Meanwhile, put the flour in a shallow bowl. Drain the artichokes well and dredge in the flour. Add the artichokes to the oil and fry until crisp, 45 seconds to 1 minute per side. Drain on paper towels. Sprinkle with salt and serve hot.

— Serves 6

Carciofi Ripieni con Pinoli e Pangrattato
Stuffed Artichokes with Pine Nuts and Breadcrumbs

Juice of 1 lemon

10 small artichokes

¼ cup extra-virgin olive oil, divided

1 small red onion, finely chopped

2 cups unseasoned dried breadcrumbs

2 tablespoons dried currants

2 tablespoons pine nuts

1 tablespoon finely chopped fresh flat-leaf parsley

2 teaspoons fine sea salt, divided

½ teaspoon red pepper flakes

1 cup white wine

1 cup water

Add the lemon juice to a large bowl filled with cold water. Trim and discard the tough outer leaves of the artichokes, then halve lengthwise and scoop out the fuzzy choke with a sharp spoon and discard. Drop the artichoke halves into the bowl of lemon water and set aside.

Combine 2 tablespoons olive oil and the onion in a medium skillet and cook over medium-high heat until softened, about 5 minutes. Reduce the heat, add the breadcrumbs, and cook, stirring often, until golden and toasted. Stir in the currants, pine nuts, parsley, 1 teaspoon salt, and red pepper flakes. Remove from the heat.

Coat the bottom of a wide, deep pan (it should be large enough for the artichokes to fit snugly without overlapping) with the remaining 2 tablespoons olive oil. Spoon the breadcrumb stuffing into the artichoke heart centers and arrange the artichokes in the pan with the filling facing up. Sprinkle with the remaining 1 teaspoon salt and cook over medium heat, 1 minute. Add the wine and water and bring to a boil. Reduce to a simmer, cover, and cook until the artichokes are tender, about 20 minutes. If the pan has too much liquid in it once the artichokes are almost fully cooked, remove the lid for the last few minutes of cooking until the liquid is reduced and syrupy.

— Serves 6

Tall and handsome, with dark hair and very bright eyes, Salvatore is caretaker number two at Case Vecchie, and substitutes for Pompeo whenever necessary, looking after the courtyard and helping Giovanni, the gardener. He loves to meet the foreign guests and is very talkative (even though he doesn't speak a word of English). Salvatore is also the man of the Vespa, the collector. One of his jobs is to go out and pick what we need in the kitchen—wild fennel, wild greens like *cavolicelli di vigna* and *sparacelli amari*, fresh almonds, and prickly pears. He comes from the hilltop town of Sclafani and has been married to Paola for many years; together, they finally have a little boy named Giuseppe.

In addition to traditional Eggplant Caponata (page 183), we also prepare an artichoke version. The artichokes are stewed rather then fried, so it is much lighter. If you have time, make this the day before; it will taste even better.

Caponata di Carciofi
Artichoke Caponata

1 small head celery, sliced

Juice of 2 lemons

4 pounds medium artichokes

¼ cup extra-virgin olive oil

1 large red onion, halved
lengthwise and thinly sliced

1 cup water, wine, or broth, or
as needed

1½ cups Salsa Pronta (page 163)
or good-quality tomato sauce

1 cup green olives, pitted and cut
lengthwise into thirds

¼ cup capers, rinsed and drained

¼ cup red or white wine vinegar

1 tablespoon sugar, or to taste

Fine sea salt

5 hard-boiled eggs, peeled and
quartered lengthwise, for garnish

¼ cup chopped fresh flat-leaf
parsley, for garnish

Cook the celery in a small pot of boiling water until crisp-tender, about 5 minutes. Drain and rinse under cold running water until cool. Drain well and set aside.

Add the lemon juice to a large bowl filled with cold water. Trim and discard the tough outer leaves of the artichokes, then halve lengthwise and scoop out the fuzzy choke with a sharp spoon and discard. Slice the artichokes into ½-inch wedges and drop into the bowl of lemon water.

Combine the olive oil and onion in a large skillet and cook over medium-high heat until golden, about 5 minutes. Add the artichokes and enough of the water to just cover. Bring to a boil, then reduce to a simmer, cover, and cook until the artichokes are tender, about 15 minutes. Stir in the tomato sauce, olives, capers, reserved celery, vinegar, sugar, and salt to taste. Simmer for 2 to 3 minutes, then transfer to a large bowl or platter and cool.

Garnish the caponata with the hard-boiled eggs and chopped parsley. Serve cold or at room temperature.

— Serves 8 to 10

When I was a child, one of the dishes our housekeeper Agostina would prepare especially for me was homemade tagliatelle with peas, diced prosciutto cotto, and lots of Parmesan. It was a classic seasoning for kids and I loved it, but the fresh pasta itself was extraordinary—slippery and light—and stuck in my mind forever.

Neither my mother nor my grandfather cared much for homemade pasta. They were huge fans of dried pasta, and not a day would pass without one if not two dishes of pasta, but very rarely was it homemade. When I joined my mother in the kitchen at Case Vecchie, I knew it was my chance to master the art of fresh pasta because all the local girls who helped out in the kitchen had that formidable skill hiding behind their smiling faces. They often prepared fresh pasta for their families' Sunday meals or special-occasion feasts. I had never made pasta myself, but I had the flavor of Agostina's tagliatelle in mind: smooth, tasting of wheat, and quite firm. Instead of peas and prosciutto, I wanted to make a very loose sauce of stewed artichokes. This is the delicious result.

Tagliatelle con Carciofi
Tagliatelle with Stewed Artichokes

PASTA

2 cups all-purpose flour

2 cups durum wheat or semolina flour

2 eggs

⅔ cup water

Pinch of fine sea salt

ARTICHOKES

Juice of 2 lemons

4 to 5 pounds small artichokes

⅓ cup extra-virgin olive oil

1 medium onion, chopped

2 garlic cloves, finely chopped

⅓ cup chopped fresh flat-leaf parsley

Fine sea salt and black pepper

¼ cup finely grated Parmesan

Make the pasta: Combine the flours, mound on a work surface, and make a well in the center. Add the eggs, water, and salt to the well and gently beat the eggs and water with a fork until combined. Gradually stir in enough flour to form a paste. Knead the remaining flour into the mixture with your hands to form a dough. Knead the dough until smooth and elastic, 8 to 10 minutes.

Set a pasta machine to the widest setting. Take a piece of dough and run it through the machine several times at that setting, folding the dough in half each time before rolling it again. When the dough is very even, continue to roll it through the machine, once at each setting without folding, until you reach the narrowest setting. Repeat with the remaining dough. Attach the tagliatelle or fettuccine attachment to the pasta machine, and feed the dough through to cut the pasta. Arrange the noodles loosely on a baking sheet dusted with semolina flour.

Prepare the artichokes: Add the lemon juice to a large bowl filled with cold water. Trim and discard the tough, outer leaves of the artichokes, then scoop out the fuzzy choke with a sharp spoon and discard. Thinly slice the artichokes and drop them in the bowl of lemon water.

Combine the olive oil, onion, and garlic in a large skillet and cook over medium heat until the onion is softened, about 5 minutes. Drain the artichokes well and add them to the skillet. Cook, stirring often, until tender, about 15 minutes. (If the artichokes are not especially tender, add a few tablespoons of water and simmer them, covered, 10 minutes.) Stir in the parsley and salt and pepper to taste.

Cook the tagliatelle in a pot of boiling well-salted water. Reserve about 1 cup of the cooking water, then drain the pasta. Combine the artichokes and the pasta in a large serving bowl, adding some of the reserved pasta cooking water if the dish is too dry. Sprinkle with the Parmesan and serve immediately.

— Serves 6

At the end of the season we also can artichokes, to have them as an appetizer for the whole year round. We remove all the tough outer leaves of very small artichokes and poach them in vinegar and water before canning them in oil. They make a wonderful appetizer in winter together with sun-dried tomatoes, stuffed peppers, and preserved mushrooms—it is a burst of heat and sun in your mouth during the chill of winter!

Carciofi sott'Olio
Preserved Artichokes

Juice of 3 lemons

4 pounds very small or baby
  artichokes

4 cups white wine vinegar

4 cups white wine

6 bay leaves, preferably fresh

2 garlic cloves, peeled

3 tablespoons fine sea salt

1 tablespoon black peppercorns

1 tablespoon coriander seeds

Vegetable oil (or a mixture of equal
  amounts vegetable and olive oils)

Add the lemon juice to a large bowl filled with cold water. Trim and discard the tough, outer leaves of the artichokes, keeping only the most tender parts. Quarter the artichokes lengthwise (if desired, scoop out the fuzzy chokes with a sharp spoon and discard) and drop them into the bowl of lemon water.

Combine the vinegar, wine, bay leaves, garlic, salt, peppercorns, and coriander in a large pot and bring to a boil. Add the artichokes and stir so they are covered. Boil for 5 minutes. Drain well, then pack the artichokes into sterilized half-pint jars. Cover with vegetable oil and screw the lids on the jars very tightly. Put the jars on a rack or a folded kitchen towel in a large pot of boiling water, and cook for 10 minutes. Remove the jars from the pot to cool completely. Store in a cool, dark place.

— Makes about 6 half-pint jars

LEGUMES

Lentils, favas, and peas are the backbone of Sicilian peasant cuisine. For centuries, these were the only proteins that poor people could afford and easily grow in their own fields. We still grow them every year, and the fava greens, left to dry in the fields, are considered an especially good way to fertilize the soil for the next season's crop. Favas and the other legumes are planted in December or January when a very cold soil protects the seeds from the insects. The seeds will start to germinate as soon as the soil starts warming up after the last freeze.

Since Case Vecchie is so close to the fields, I can look out my window and see when the favas are ready to be picked. In early May, we harvest the small favas to make *frittella*, a braised dish that is often made with artichokes. When the beans are small, the peel is so tender we don't bother to remove it. By the end of May, the big favas are ready. These will need to be peeled, a job we often do sitting out in the courtyard if the weather is nice. The beans leave a gluey stickiness on your hands while you peel them, but they are delicious to eat raw—crunchy and slightly bitter. We poach and freeze the peeled favas so we can make Macco (page 90) all year round.

The care and labor that are dedicated to the peeling and storage of favas make it clear that favas have a significant place in our diet, as well as in our traditions. For instance, for the feast of Sant'Agata on February 5, pastry shops in Catania still prepare *le favuzze di Sant'Agata*, almond paste treats that have been carefully molded to look like tiny green fava beans.

Frittella con Carciofi e Fave
Frittella with Artichokes and Fava Beans

Juice of 1 lemon

4 medium artichokes

½ cup extra-virgin olive oil

1 small red onion, chopped

2 heaping cups shelled fresh or frozen fava beans, blanched and peeled

Fine sea salt

½ cup warm water

Add the lemon juice to a large bowl filled with cold water. Trim and discard the tough outer leaves of the artichokes, then scoop out the fuzzy choke with a sharp spoon and discard. Cut the artichokes into ⅛- to ¼-inch-thick slices, and drop into the bowl of lemon water.

Combine the olive oil and onion in a medium saucepan and cook over medium heat until softened, about 5 minutes. Add the favas and a large pinch of salt and cook 1 to 2 minutes more. Add the artichokes and the ½ cup warm water, cover, and simmer gently until the favas and artichokes are tender, 20 to 30 minutes. If mixture is too liquidy near the end of cooking, uncover to evaporate while cooking.

— Serves 4

Eggs and favas are an extraordinary match. I like to serve Macco (page 90) with a loosely poached egg on top so that the yolk breaks into the soup, flavoring the dense fava bean puree. This frittata combines similar ingredients in a very different way. There is no tradition behind it; one day I just put together two flavors I love, and I've been making it ever since.

Frittata con Fave
Frittata with Fava Beans

2 tablespoons extra-virgin olive oil

1 small red onion, finely chopped

2 heaping cups shelled fresh or
    frozen fava beans, blanched and
    peeled

¾ cup water

1¼ teaspoons fine sea salt, divided

4 eggs

3 heaping tablespoons finely grated
    Parmesan

¼ teaspoon red pepper flakes

Combine the olive oil and onion in a medium nonstick skillet and cook over medium heat until softened, about 5 minutes. Add the favas and cook, stirring occasionally, 1 to 2 minutes. Stir in the water and 1 teaspoon salt, cover, and simmer until most of the water has evaporated, 10 to 15 minutes. Meanwhile, beat the eggs with the Parmesan, red pepper flakes, and remaining ¼ teaspoon salt in a small bowl. Once most of the water has evaporated from the pan, add the egg mixture and cook until the bottom of the frittata has set but the top is still runny. Remove from the heat and cover the pan. Let stand, until the top has just set and the eggs are cooked, about 5 minutes.

— Serves 4

Looking at pebbly brown lentils, you would never imagine that the lentil harvest is one of the most poetic moments in our agricultural life. Many farms hire a machine to do the work, but those who grow small quantities of lentils still do it by hand. When the plants are ready to be harvested, Carmelo cuts them down and leaves them to dry on a big tarp laid out on the ground. After a few days (which are spent hoping it won't rain!), Carmelo beats the dried plants with a long, thick stick so that the lentils fall from their pods, and then he scoops up the dried plants with a pitchfork and tosses them in the air so that all the dried seeds fall out and collect on the tarp. Finally, the lentils must be shaken through a sieve so that all the twigs and bits of chaff are removed. It is hard and sweaty work, but magical to watch.

There are at least twenty different varieties of lentils in Sicily. We grow two types at Regaleali: a very small, dark brown specimen from Ustica and the so-called Villalba lentil, named for a nearby village. This flat, greenish brown lentil was introduced to the area in the nineteenth century by a group of Sicilian peasants escaping a cruel landlord in Palma di Montechiaro. Our lentils require soaking before being cooked for this salad, but I know that most green lentils available in North American markets—which will work fine in this recipe—do not need this extra step.

Insalata di Lenticchie con Menta e Scorzetta di Arancia
Lentil Salad with Mint and Orange Zest

2 cups green lentils (not Le Puy)

3 tablespoons extra-virgin olive oil

Juice of 1 lemon

Leaves from 1 large bunch fresh mint, finely chopped

2 teaspoons dried oregano, preferably wild

Finely grated zest of 1 orange

Fine sea salt

Cover the lentils with 4 cups cold water in a medium saucepan. Bring to a boil, then reduce to a simmer, cover, and cook until tender, about 20 minutes. Drain the lentils and cool.

In a bowl, combine the lentils with the olive oil, lemon juice, oregano, mint, orange zest, and salt to taste. Serve chilled or at room temperature.

— Serves 6

Zuppa di Lenticchie
Lentil Soup

¼ cup extra-virgin olive oil

1 red onion, chopped

3½ cups green lentils (not Le Puy)

12 cups water

3 small carrots, chopped

1 celery stalk or 1 small bunch
celery leaves, chopped

½ cup wild fennel, chopped
(optional)

Pinch of dried oregano,
preferably wild

Fine sea salt and black pepper

1 cup ditalini or other small
dried pasta

Combine the olive oil and onion in a large pot and cook over medium heat until softened, about 5 minutes. Add the lentils and stir to coat with oil. Add the water, carrots, celery, and wild fennel (if using). Bring to a boil, then reduce heat and simmer, covered, until lentils and vegetables are tender, 40 to 45 minutes. Season with the oregano and salt and pepper to taste.

Meanwhile, cook the pasta in a small pot of boiling well-salted water. Drain well and stir into the soup.

— Serves 10

TUNA

Every once in awhile, I get a call from my friend Franco il Pescatore with the news that he is coming to Case Vecchie with a couple of big tunas for us to play with. I have known this spectacular, generous man since I was a child. Like all the men from Porticello, a small town on the coast half an hour from Palermo, Franco is the son of a fisherman. Bucking tradition, he moved to Palermo and started working as a butler in my Uncle Gioacchino's house, then he got a job at a private club where he met all the Palermitan aristocratic families. Now he owns a good restaurant in Porticello, and though he speaks only a few words of English, he nevertheless travels all over, meeting friends and relatives who have emigrated to different parts of the globe, even teaching housekeepers in Japan how to cook Italian and Sicilian dishes. He used to visit my mother and now he visits me, always with a lovely, fishy gift from Porticello. When Franco pulls up to Case Vecchie, I know that the day will be a whole tuna celebration, with Franco as the principal actor and Giovanna and me hanging around the table, ready to anticipate his wishes!

Tuna, Franco says, is like pork: Nothing gets wasted. The heads and the fins are used to make a tuna ragù that will be frozen for later; the tuna roe makes a fabulous topping for pasta, and finally, my favorite part, the tuna sperm dipped in batter and fried becomes a wonderful antipasto. The rest of the tuna will be canned, except for a few steaks that I marinate in olive oil, then dredge in breadcrumbs and grill, just like Pesce Spada Impanato (page 200).

Home-canned tuna has a very special place in my heart—for me, it is the equivalent of Proust's madeleine. When my cousins and I headed to the north of Italy for our university studies, every six months my grandmother would send up a truck stuffed with food for the "exiles" (that was the only way my grandmother could think of us when we were far from home). Among the crates of wine, homemade tomato sauce, and canned caponata, there might be a few jars of tuna made by Mario in my grandmother's kitchen. The cans of tuna were so precious that a sort of improvised trade sprung up among the cousins, more wine for two cans of tuna or a few jars of caponata for tuna, and so on. Not surprisingly, I was the one who would usually give up wine for extra tuna.

We prepare a great quantity of canned tuna at one time. No matter the quantities, the important thing is to maintain the proportion of salt and water, since the salt is what helps preserve the tuna; figure on about 1 tablespoon salt per quart of water. I find that this tuna keeps for several months in a cool, dark place, but if you prefer, it can also be stored in the refrigerator.

Tonno sott'Olio
Canned Tuna

4 pounds fresh albacore tuna, cut into thick steaks

1 tablespoon fine sea salt

1 tablespoon red or white wine vinegar

Vegetable oil, for canning

Combine the tuna and salt with 4 cups water in a large pot and bring to a boil, covered, over medium-high heat. When it comes to a boil, add the vinegar, reduce to a simmer, and cook, uncovered, until the tuna is fully cooked and has turned a light shade of pink, 15 to 20 minutes.

Remove the tuna from the cooking liquid, and arrange on a baking sheet. Cover with a dish towel and refrigerate for at least 10 hours, or overnight.

The next day, remove and discard any skin and bones and gently break the meat into 2- to 3-inch chunks. Place the meat into sterilized glass jars and cover completely with vegetable oil. Let the tuna soak in the oil for at least 30 minutes, then add more oil to refill the jars almost to the top.

Screw the lids on the jars very tightly. Put the jars on a rack or a folded kitchen towel in a large pot of cold water, bring to a boil, and cook for 1 hour, timed from when you turn on the heat. Remove from the heat and let the jars sit in the water for 30 minutes longer, then remove from the pot to cool completely. Store in a cool, dark place or in the refrigerator.

— *Makes about 5 pint jars*

My favorite way to serve the canned tuna is to strain it from the oil and set it on a large platter. Peel and slice a few boiled potatoes, and arrange them around the tuna. Drizzle everything with plenty of good extra-virgin olive oil and sprinkle with chopped parsley and some black pepper. A good aïoli completes the dish.

Il Mio Aïoli
My Aïoli

1 garlic clove, chopped

Fine sea salt

1 teaspoon Dijon mustard, plus
  more to taste

1 egg yolk, at room temperature

1 cup vegetable oil

¼ cup extra-virgin olive oil

Juice of ½ lemon

1 teaspoon red wine vinegar

Using a mortar and pestle, pound the garlic with a pinch of salt until mashed into a very smooth paste. Pound in the mustard until smooth and combined. Pound in the egg yolk until thick and sticky. Stir together the vegetable and olive oils, then add the oils, drop by drop, while constantly pounding and blending. When the sauce has thickened to the consistency of heavy cream, switch from the pestle to a whisk and continue to add the oil in a thin stream, whisking constantly. When all the oil is added and the mixture is smooth and creamy, stir in the lemon juice and vinegar. Season with more salt and mustard to taste.

Note: The egg yolk in this recipe is not cooked. If salmonella is a concern in your area and you are at risk, do not make this recipe.

— Makes about 1½ cups

I also use canned tuna as a stuffing for cherry peppers, but I must point out that all my ancestors would roll over in their graves if I used homemade canned tuna—it's too precious!—for this recipe. Instead, I call for a good-quality store-bought canned tuna that is packed in oil. This is a recipe that you need to taste your way through, since different brands of canned tuna, anchovies, and capers have varying levels of saltiness. These peppers are delicious served immediately as an antipasto.

Peperoncini Ripieni
Cherry Peppers Stuffed with Tuna

1 pound cherry peppers

1 cup white wine

1 cup white wine vinegar

2 teaspoons sugar

2 garlic cloves, peeled and smashed

5 whole cloves

2 bay leaves, preferably fresh

Two (5-ounce) cans oil-packed tuna, not drained

12 green olives, pitted and chopped

2 tablespoons capers, rinsed and chopped

2 anchovy fillets, finely chopped

Cut the tops off the cherry peppers and carefully remove the seeds. Wash and set on a towel to dry.

Combine the wine, vinegar, sugar, garlic, cloves, and bay leaves in a medium saucepan. Bring to a boil over medium-high heat, then add the peppers. Reduce the heat and cook, covered, until just tender, about 10 minutes. Drain (discard the cooking liquid and spices) and cool.

With a fork, mash together the tuna, olives, capers, and anchovies. Stuff the cooled peppers with the tuna mixture.

— Serves 6 to 8

Franco introduced me to fried tuna sperm, and it is one of the most special things I've ever tasted. The texture and flavor are unbelievable and really have nothing to do with fish. I would describe it as closer to calf's brains. It stays firm under its breadcrumb coating and then bursts in your mouth when you take a bite.

Lattume di Tonno Fritto
Fried Tuna Sperm

2 eggs, beaten

1 tablespoon finely chopped fresh
   flat-leaf parsley

1 teaspoon fine sea salt

½ teaspoon black pepper

2 cups unseasoned dried
   breadcrumbs

10 ounces tuna sperm sac

Vegetable oil, for frying

Mix together the eggs, parsley, salt, and pepper in a bowl. Place the breadcrumbs in another bowl. Cut the sperm sac diagonally into pieces, about ¼ inch thick. Dip each piece first into the egg mixture and then dredge in the breadcrumbs.

Heat 2 inches of oil in a large heavy skillet. Add the breaded sperm pieces, in batches, and fry until golden brown, about 1 minute per side. Drain on paper towels. Sprinkle with salt and serve hot.

— Serves 6

Tuna roe makes for a deliciously fishy pasta sauce. The roe breaks up in the sauce and produces a sort of granular yet creamy consistency, while the addition of garlic and white wine enhances the notes of salinity and wildness. You can substitute canned tuna for the roe; the texture will be chunky and very different, but it will also taste very good. The roe has a more pungent tuna flavor, which pairs very well with a glass of ice-cold white wine.

Spaghetti con Uova di Tonno Fresche
Spaghetti with Tuna Roe

1 pound tuna roe sack or three (5-ounce) cans oil-packed tuna

½ cup extra-virgin olive oil

3 garlic cloves, minced

½ cup white wine

1 teaspoon red pepper flakes

1 teaspoon fine sea salt

½ teaspoon black pepper

7 cups canned Roma (plum) tomatoes, passed through a food mill

1 teaspoon sugar

¼ cup finely chopped fresh flat-leaf parsley

¼ cup finely chopped fresh mint leaves

1 pound dried pasta, such as spaghetti, linguine, or bucatini

To remove the roe from the sack, make a vertical incision into the outer layer of the sack, then carefully "open" the sack so that it lies flat with the outer layer against your work surface and the roe exposed on top. With a knife, gently scrape out the roe, discarding the sack.

Combine the olive oil and garlic in a large skillet and cook over medium heat until the garlic is softened, about 2 minutes. Add the roe and cook until browned, stirring constantly. Add the wine, red pepper flakes, salt, and black pepper, and cook 1 minute more. Add the tomatoes and sugar and simmer, uncovered, until slightly thickened, about 5 minutes. Remove from the heat and stir in the parsley and mint.

Meanwhile, cook the pasta in a large pot of boiling well-salted water. Toss with the sauce and serve immediately.

— Serves 6

Any waste that comes from canning the tuna, what we call the *murlane*, goes into making a tasty ragù. Ask your fishmonger for extra bits and pieces, like the head, jowls, tail, and bones.

Ragù di Tonno
Tuna Ragù

½ cup extra-virgin olive oil

1 medium onion, coarsely chopped

2½ pounds tuna pieces, such as the head, jowls, tail, and bones

½ cup red or white wine

2 tablespoons *estratto* or good-quality sun-dried tomato paste

4 cups water

1 tablespoon dried oregano, preferably wild

1 teaspoon fine sea salt

½ teaspoon black pepper

Combine the olive oil and onion in a large pot and cook over medium-high heat until softened, about 5 minutes. Add the tuna pieces and cook for 3 minutes more. Add the wine and cook 2 minutes more.

Stir the *estratto* into the water until dissolved, then add it to the pot along with the oregano, salt, and pepper. Reduce the heat to medium and cook until the sauce has come together and a bold tuna flavor is present, about 1 hour. Remove the head and any bones, then pass the sauce through a food mill or a fine-mesh sieve. Either serve immediately with pasta or store in the refrigerator or freezer for later use.

— *Makes about 2 cups*

SARDINES

Sardines have always been a big business in Sicily. When the female sardines are pregnant in winter and spring, huge schools swim close to the coast, practically floating on the surface of the sea, so they are very easy for fishermen to net. I often cook with fresh sardines, but have found that Americans are a bit suspicious of them because they have only had canned sardines, which may have such a strong flavor. But if sardines are very fresh, you will be amazed by how sweet they are, not at all fishy. When Franco comes to Case Vecchie, he sometimes brings along some baby sardines, which he coats with semolina flour and deep-fries. Even better are *sarde allinguate*, fried sardines that have first been marinated in red wine vinegar—exquisite!

Sarde Allinguate
Fried Vinegar Sardines

1 pound very fresh small sardines, heads removed, cleaned, and deboned

1 cup red wine vinegar

2 to 3 cups semolina flour

Vegetable oil, for frying

Fine sea salt

Put the sardines in a shallow baking dish, cover with the vinegar, and marinate for 15 to 20 minutes. Fill a shallow bowl with the flour. Drain the sardines and dredge lightly in the flour.

Heat 1 inch of oil in a large heavy skillet. Add the sardines and fry until golden, 1 to 2 minutes. Drain on paper towels. Sprinkle with salt and serve hot.

— Serves 6 to 8

Lots of restaurants in Sicily serve anchovies marinated in vinegar, but the vinegar is often very harsh and the fish rather muddy tasting. One summer on the island of Pantelleria, I learned how to marinate all sorts of seafood—sardines, shrimp, octopus—mostly with good, fresh lemon juice, which is how I came up with my "sushi" sardines. I like to serve them on slices of toasted bread. They are much fresher and more pulpy than those restaurant-style anchovies and a nice contrast to the Sarde Allinguate (page 137).

Sarde Marinate
Citrus-Marinated Sardines

½ pound very fresh small sardines, heads removed, cleaned, and deboned

Juice of 2 lemons

Juice of 1 orange

1 small loaf good-quality semolina bread, thinly sliced

1 garlic clove, halved

¼ cup extra-virgin olive oil

1 tablespoon dried oregano, preferably wild

Fine sea salt and black pepper

Place the sardines in a small bowl and cover with the lemon and orange juices. Marinate for 20 to 30 minutes.

Meanwhile, preheat the broiler. Arrange the bread on a baking sheet and broil, flipping halfway through, until lightly toasted, about 3 minutes.

In a small bowl, combine the garlic, olive oil, oregano, and salt to taste. Drain the sardines, then dip each in the olive oil mixture and serve on the toasted bread, sprinkled with salt and pepper.

— Serves 8

Sarde a beccafico might be the prettiest dish we make. We arrange the shiny sardines so their tails are all flipping in the same direction and tuck bay leaves and thin slices of orange and lemon among the fish. People who claim they don't like sardines are always surprised by how much they love this dish.

Sarde a Beccafico
Sardines Stuffed with Breadcrumbs and Currants

¼ cup extra-virgin olive oil, plus more for drizzling

1 small red onion, very finely chopped

½ cup unseasoned dried breadcrumbs

¼ cup dried currants

¼ cup pine nuts

¼ cup finely chopped fresh flat-leaf parsley

¼ cup finely chopped fresh mint leaves

Juice of 1 lemon, plus ½ lemon, very thinly sliced

Fine sea salt and black pepper

2 pounds very fresh small sardines, heads removed, cleaned, and deboned

½ orange, very thinly sliced

12 bay leaves, preferably fresh

Combine ¼ cup olive oil and the onion in a small skillet and cook over medium heat until just golden, about 5 minutes. Stir in the breadcrumbs and cook until toasted, about 2 minutes. Stir in the currants, pine nuts, parsley, and mint. Remove from the heat. Add the lemon juice and salt and pepper to taste, and mix well. Cool.

Preheat the oven to 375°F. Lightly oil a ceramic baking dish.

Lay a sardine skin-side down, with the tail facing away from you, on a work surface. Put about 1½ teaspoons filling on the bottom third of the sardine, then roll up. Repeat with remaining sardines and filling. Arrange the sardines with their tails sticking up, all in the same direction and close together, in the baking dish. Place the slices of lemon and orange and the bay leaves decoratively between the sardines, and drizzle with olive oil. Bake until tender, 15 to 20 minutes. Serve warm or at room temperature.

— Serves 6

SUMMER

Summer explodes in Sicily like a mouthful of orange— overpoweringly sweet, lazy, sexy. When it is too warm to travel by car, I sometimes take the train from Palermo to the tiny station in Vallelunga, the village closest to Case Vecchie. The two-wagon train gently follows the coastline toward Cefalù and then, at Cerda, abruptly snakes into the interior, away from the sparkling sea.

From a seat near the wide windows, I can study the sunburned landscape where the golden fields of wheat and straw are interrupted by dashes of red poppies, prickly blue cardoons, and yellow broom. I know the fields will soon darken to black when the farmers burn their fields to fertilize the soil after the harvest. Regaleali is a welcome exception to these stark colors; the intensely green grapevines look like decadent ladies stretching their arms. By August, it will be time to start picking tomatoes, eggplants, peppers, watermelons, figs, and zucchini—all the juicy, watery fruits and vegetables that help us deal with the big heat of summer.

Now is the moment to crawl up the hills above Villalba to collect wild oregano. No recipe in the world is better than good fresh bread toasted and dipped in olive oil mixed with salt, and plenty of dried wild oregano. My cousins and I often ate this as a main dish during childhood visits to my Aunt Costanza's house in Pantelleria. We would fill a stone hollowed out by the sea's waves with our oily mixture and then dip the bread in. Now, I like to pack the precious mixture with me when I take guests to picnic at the ancient garden of Kolymbetra, which lies in the heart of the Valley of the Temples in Agrigento. We eat it with a sort of flatbread called *muffolette*, which is made by Pompeo's sister Franca, a baker in Vallelunga.

Bruschetta con Olio e Origano
Bruschette with Olive Oil and Dried Oregano

1 small loaf good-quality semolina
 bread, thinly sliced

1 cup extra-virgin olive oil

¼ cup dried oregano, preferably wild

1 teaspoon fine sea salt, or to taste

Preheat the broiler. Arrange the bread on a baking sheet and broil, flipping halfway through, until lightly toasted, about 3 minutes. Meanwhile, stir together the olive oil, oregano, and salt in a wide bowl. Dip the warm bread completely into the olive oil mixture and serve immediately.

— Serves 8

ALMONDS

Old almond trees, crippled, nearly abandoned, but still generous, are found all over Sicily. The trees often produce nuts that are ugly, wrinkled, and very dark. Some are small, some are large, but when they are fresh, they taste of milk and earth. When they are dried, there is always a hint of dust in them, as well as a stronger almond flavor. Sicilians use almonds at every stage of growth, even before they ripen. When almonds are in that green, juicy state, we transform them into a liqueur known as *mandorlino*, after that, pesto, then almond paste, almond milk, *semifreddo* . . . and so on, up to frying them in their brown skins and serving them as an accompaniment to cocktails.

My mother was very fond of *nocino*, a walnut liqueur that is made all over Italy, and used to make it every year. Today, we still harvest the green walnuts in June and steep them with spices in alcohol in big glass jars that sit in a sunny corner of my balcony. By July, when the hottest days of summer hit, the *nocino* is ready to be strained and bottled. The idea of making the almond version, which seems more Sicilian to me, came up one day while I was preparing the *nocino* with Giovanna. I followed the *nocino* recipe, substituting unripe almonds and their fuzzy green peels, which are sometimes chewed on by people working on the land to get some moisture. I was able to achieve a very fresh-tasting liqueur, densely perfumed and with a beautiful light-amber color. My father, who usually cares only for whisky and cognac, loved it!

Mandorlino
Green Almond Liqueur

2 (750 ml) bottles 95-proof grain alcohol

6 cups water

5½ cups sugar

60 fresh green almonds with green peel, halved

1 lemon, quartered

1 cinnamon stick

1 tablespoon whole cloves

1 tablespoon coriander seeds

Combine all the ingredients in a large glass container with a tight-fitting lid. Stir together until the sugar dissolves, then place in a warm, sunny place, preferably outdoors, and let stand for forty days. Strain the liqueur through a fine-mesh sieve into bottles and cover tightly. Store in a cool, dry place.

Note: You can make Nocino *the same way as* Mandorlino. *Simply substitute an equal amount of green walnuts, halved.*

— Makes about 4 quarts

My grandmother Franca was known for giving splendid dinner parties. In the summer, she would offer a small bowl of fresh almonds floating in salted water at the end of the meal—so simple but, to my mind, so luxurious. When harvested in June, the almonds are enrobed by a bright green shell, which you can crack easily with your teeth. A thin yellow skin covers the almond itself; it must be peeled off to reveal the crisp, snow-white nut. If dunked in salted water for a while, the peel slides off easily, and eating them is like rattling off the rosary—you pop one after another into your mouth without stopping.

One of the best things to do with fresh almonds is make pesto. As my Ligurian friend Maria Flora Giubilei says, only Ligurians follow strict rules when making pesto; to everyone else, pesto is a subjective matter. For instance, every Sicilian has his own way of making *pesto alla trapanese*. I personally like to encounter big chunks of almonds and tomatoes in a mouthful of spaghetti. So I puree the basil with the olive oil, grind the almonds coarsely, and then gently stir in some coarsely chopped ripe tomatoes.

Pesto alla Trapanese
Pesto with Almonds and Fresh Tomatoes

4 cups loosely packed basil leaves

1 cup extra-virgin olive oil

1 large garlic clove, coarsely chopped

1 teaspoon fine sea salt

1 cup whole blanched almonds

1 medium tomato, peeled and chopped into ½-inch pieces

Combine the basil, olive oil, garlic, and salt in a food processor, and puree until very smooth. Add the almonds and pulse until coarsely chopped. Transfer to a bowl and stir in the tomatoes.

— Makes about 2 cups

Sage is so beautiful, generous, and resistant to our unpredictable weather that I have taken to planting different varieties all over my garden. It also makes a marvelous pesto, with either fresh or dried almonds, which is delicious with Ravioli Stuffed with Ricotta and Mint (page 74). I find it respects the delicacy of the pasta.

Pesto di Mandorle e Salvia
Almond and Sage Pesto

1 cup whole blanched almonds

2 cups loosely packed fresh
   sage leaves

1 large garlic clove, coarsely chopped

1 teaspoon fine sea salt

1½ cups extra-virgin olive oil

Process the almonds in a food processor until finely ground. Add the sage, garlic, and salt, and process to a paste. Add the olive oil little by little, grinding between each addition until the pesto comes together into a smooth sauce.

— Makes about 1½ cups

The difference between marzipan and almond paste, which in Sicily we call *pasta reale*, has been a puzzle to me since I was a child. Nobody in my family could give me an answer. Finally, my Aunt Costanza pointed me in the direction of an unpretentious little pastry shop in Favara, east of Agrigento. With no sign or windows on the street, it's the kind of place you had to know about beforehand, otherwise you would never find it. For years, this was where my aunt, possibly the most gluttonous person in a family of gluttons, would buy one or two almond paste sheep for Easter. Pastry shops all over Sicily sell these little edible sculptures, but the ones from Favara are special: Their almond coats hide a center made of pistachio paste, quite a marvelous combination.

I knew that if I went to the shop without an introduction, I would be met with mumbles, so my aunt made a phone call and asked if I could observe them at work. Their desire for secrecy is understandable, since their recipe is a unique one, apparently handed down by a nun related to the family. When I arrived, ten women of all ages were working together, producing pounds and pounds of almond and pistachio pastes, in a kitchen equipped with only one stove, a small food processor, and lots of energy. But all work stopped and ten pairs of eyes turned to stare at me when I started asking about the marzipan sheep. "Marzipan?! How dare you talk about marzipan?" the eldest lady seemed to say with a fierce glance, while another explained, "This is *pasta reale*. It has nothing to do with marzipan, which is made with uncooked almonds and breaks up as soon as you try to mold it!" While she talked, she rolled and shaped small balls of almond paste, demonstrating how malleable it was compared to the marzipan I usually make for cassata. Their paste was beautifully moist and elastic, and you could work with it as if it were clay. I watched carefully, but of course the recipe was hidden behind their words and I dared not ask for it. I couldn't possibly expect to figure out a recipe after one visit, but after many more chats and several flocks of sheep, here is what I have come up with.

Pasta Reale
Almond Paste

2⅔ cups whole almonds   ½ cup water

1⅓ cups granulated sugar   Powdered sugar

Bring a large pot of water to a boil. Add the almonds and boil until they float to the surface. Skim off any foam from the surface, then drain in a colander. When the almonds have cooled slightly, peel off their skins and discard.

Preheat the oven to its lowest possible temperature. Spread the almonds on a baking sheet and bake, moving the almonds around with your hands occasionally, until dried, 10 to 15 minutes. Cool completely.

Working in very small batches, grind the cooled almonds with a big pinch of the granulated sugar until very fine and powdery. Transfer the ground almonds to a medium saucepan, along with the remaining granulated sugar. Stir to combine. Add the water, and cook over medium-low heat, stirring constantly, until the mixture has thickened to the consistency of polenta and the sugar is dissolved, 5 to 10 minutes.

Dust a cold work surface, such as marble, with powdered sugar. Transfer the almond paste to the work surface to cool. Roll the cooled almond paste into the shapes you wish, dusting with more powdered sugar as needed. Store in an airtight container in the refrigerator.

— Makes about 3 cups

I've never been fond of coffee, especially in Sicily where it is a dense brown liquid that is served boiling hot and very strong! I have always preferred black or smoked English tea. But a few years ago I decided to cut out caffeine completely. Because I am constantly planting new herbs, I started making my own herbal tea blends from the aromatic plants in my garden. I like to sweeten the tea with a few leaves of fresh stevia, which is a fabulous natural sweetener. This is my favorite combination: Combine 5 sprigs fresh peppermint, 1 sprig fresh lemon verbena, and 1 small sprig stevia in a teapot. Pour 4 cups boiling water into the pot and steep for 5 minutes.

I use *pasta reale* as the base for a very refreshing granita. It is very delicate, with the almond flavor blooming at the end. A drizzle of vino cotto adds a welcome touch of sweetness. I know it is not traditional, but I like to make my granita in an ice cream maker; it produces a much finer texture than the kind you scrape by hand, and the vino cotto blends in beautifully.

Granita alle Mandorle con Vino Cotto
Almond Granita with Vino Cotto

¾ cup Pasta Reale (page 154)

½ cup sugar

4 cups water

Vino cotto, for serving

Combine the almond paste, sugar, and water in a large bowl and stir until paste and sugar are dissolved. Pour the mixture into a large metal baking pan and freeze, stirring with a fork, every 30 minutes, until the mixture is firm, but not frozen hard, 3 to 4 hours. Before serving, scrape the granita with a fork to lighten the texture. (Alternatively, freeze the mixture in an ice cream maker.) Serve drizzled with a spoonful of vino cotto.

— Makes about 1 quart

Beppa, the cook at my mother-in-law's house, was a master at making semifreddo. While I was married to Luca, I started making it, too, but it was always frustrating because it could never, ever be as good as Beppa's. But when I started at the cooking school, developing this new *semifreddo* with a Sicilian vibe was my sweet revenge!

Semifreddo di Mandorle e Pistacchio
Almond and Pistachio Semifreddo

1 cup whole almonds, coarsely chopped

¾ cup shelled pistachios, coarsely chopped

1½ cups plus 3 tablespoons sugar, divided

3 eggs, separated (see note below)

2 cups heavy cream

Combine the almonds, pistachios, and 1 cup sugar in a medium saucepan and cook over medium-low heat, stirring occasionally (more frequently toward the end), until the nuts are caramelized and deep golden brown, about 8 minutes. Remove from the heat and spread the nuts out on a plate to cool.

Combine the egg yolks and ½ cup sugar in a bowl. With an electric mixer, beat the mixture until thick and pale golden, about 10 minutes. Set aside.

Combine the egg whites and 2 tablespoons sugar in another bowl and beat with the cleaned mixer until stiff peaks form. Set aside.

Combine the cream and remaining 1 tablespoon sugar in a large bowl and beat with the cleaned mixer until soft peaks form.

Break up the candied nuts, then gently fold them into the whipped cream with a rubber spatula. Once combined, fold in the yolk mixture, then gently fold in the egg whites. Spoon the mixture into a large metal bowl (or 2 loaf pans) and rap the bottom on a work surface several times to get rid of any air bubbles. Freeze at least 8 hours or overnight. To unmold, dip the bottom of the bowl in warm water, then invert onto a serving platter.

Note: The eggs in this recipe are not cooked. If salmonella is a concern in your area and you are at risk, do not make this recipe.

— Serves 10

Regaleali's general manager, Gaetano Maccarrone, was born in the eastern part of Sicily where, until recently, kids usually drank almond milk for breakfast because it was more available than dairy milk. He shared this recipe with me. Chilled, it makes a very refreshing morning drink.

Latte di Mandorle
Fresh Almond Milk

2 cups whole almonds

6 cups water

3 tablespoons sugar, or to taste

Bring a large pot of water to a boil. Add the almonds and boil until they float to the surface. Skim off any foam from the surface, then drain in a colander. When the almonds have cooled slightly, peel off their skins and discard.

Transfer the almonds to a food processor and pulse until finely chopped (but not fully ground). Put half the almonds on a clean tea towel and place the towel over a large bowl. Slowly pour 1 cup cold water into the towel, then squeeze the almonds enclosed in the towel until the cloudy milk drips into the bowl. Continue adding water and squeezing until the milk runs clear (you should use about 3 cups water). Discard the almonds and repeat the process with the rest of the almonds and water. Add the sugar to taste and stir until dissolved. Refrigerate and serve cold.

— Makes about 5 cups

TOMATOES

The last weeks of August, when the days are sunny and dry, is the time when Sicilian housekeepers must put up all the tomato sauce that they will need for the upcoming year. During our own tomato frenzy, Case Vecchie's courtyard becomes splattered with red from all the tomatoes that we are canning in various ways. But before we begin, Giovanna and I must sit down together to figure out exactly how many bottles of tomato sauce, or *salsa pronta*, we need to make, as well as the number of jars of *polpa più* (chopped tomatoes) and *estratto* (sun-dried tomato paste). It looks like we are mapping out a war strategy or preparing for a famine! But in fact, every bottle of tomato sauce—and we make more than one hundred each year—will be accounted for. Some of it goes to Palermo for my father and me, some to Ruggero in Milan and to Virginia in Bologna, but most of it is reserved for use at Case Vecchie, for our everyday life and our cooking classes.

We use mostly Roma tomatoes that we buy from local growers for our sauce. This tomato, also known as *pomodoro seccagno*, is quite dry, dense, and deeply red. It grows happily in the clayish soil in the area around Regaleali and needs very little water. Before Giovanna's arrival, the sauce was cooked on the wood stove that we used to make ricotta, but now we find it more practical to set up big camping burners in the ancient storeroom behind the kitchen, where all the tractors are parked. We start by cooking whole tomatoes with some seasonings in giant pots. A small amount of water added to the pot keeps the tomatoes from burning, and we take turns stirring them to help break them up. Once they have broken down to a rough puree, we run them through an electric food mill and then cook the puree some more to thicken it. We cook one hundred pounds of tomatoes at a time and then repeat this process at least three times. It all looks rather Dante-esque, but it works!

Salsa Pronta
Tomato Sauce

5 pounds Roma (plum) tomatoes

1 cup water

2 large red onions, coarsely chopped, divided

3 bay leaves, preferably fresh

4 garlic cloves, peeled, divided

½ cup extra-virgin olive oil

Leaves from 1 large bunch basil

1 tablespoon fine sea salt, or to taste

1 tablespoon sugar, or to taste

Combine the tomatoes and water in a large pot. Add half the red onions, the bay leaves, and 2 garlic cloves. Bring to a boil, then reduce to a simmer, cover, and cook until the tomatoes split and begin to break up, about 20 minutes (stir frequently to keep from sticking). Continue to simmer, covered, stirring frequently, until the mixture becomes a rough puree, about 20 minutes more. Remove from the heat and pass the puree through a food mill to separate the skins from the tomatoes.

Combine the olive oil, basil leaves, remaining onion, and remaining 2 garlic cloves in a blender or food processor and puree until very smooth. Transfer the tomato puree and the basil puree into a large cleaned pot and cook over medium heat, uncovered, until slightly thickened, 20 to 30 minutes (not too stiff; you want this to be a tomato sauce, not a paste). Remove from the heat and stir in the salt and sugar to taste. Cool. The sauce can be canned (if canning, pour the sauce into sterilized jars or bottles while it is still hot) or stored in the refrigerator or freezer until ready to use.

— Makes about 8 cups

Other than spaghetti, one of the best ways to use this tomato sauce is with poached eggs. We call this dish *uova alla vastasa*, which means "vulgar eggs," because it is made of next to nothing. The wonderful flavor comes from the egg yolk dripping into the homemade tomato sauce, perfect with a hunk of good bread. Sometimes I like to sprinkle some chopped basil or oregano over the finished dish. My father pretends he does not like this simple meal, but in fact every bite disappears when I make it for him.

Uova alla Vastasa
Eggs Poached in Tomato Sauce

2 cups Salsa Pronta (page 163)   2 eggs
    or good-quality tomato sauce   Fine sea salt

Cook the tomato sauce in a medium skillet over medium heat until the sauce thickens enough that you can make two "wells" in it. Crack 1 egg into each well and season with salt. Reduce the heat to low, cover, and cook until the egg whites are set. Serve immediately.

— *Serves 1*

Uova a trippa is the elegant counterpoint to *uova alla vastasa*. I have never seen this casserole of egg ribbons layered with tomato sauce outside of my family's house. It was one of Mario's recipes and is a perfect example of his brand of haute cuisine. My son, Ruggero, especially loves this dish and always seems to ask for it when it is 90 degrees outside and too hot to think about standing over a stove making crêpe after crêpe.

Uova a Trippa
Egg Ribbons

4 eggs

⅔ cup all-purpose flour

1 cup whole milk

½ teaspoon fine sea salt

Butter

2 cups Salsa Pronta (page 163) or good-quality tomato sauce

½ pound fresh mozzarella, coarsely grated or sliced

⅓ cup grated Parmesan, plus more for serving

Beat the eggs in a medium bowl, then whisk in the flour, a little at a time. Whisk in the milk and salt until smooth and well combined.

Grease a 9-inch nonstick crêpe or omelet pan with butter and heat it over medium heat. When the pan is hot, pour in about ⅓ cup batter and swirl to coat, making a thick crêpe. Cook until the top sets, about 1 minute, then flip and cook the other side, about 30 seconds more. Transfer the crêpe to a plate and repeat with remaining batter. Stack the crêpes and cut them into ½-inch strips. Set aside.

Preheat the oven to 350°F. Grease a 12-by-9-inch baking dish.

Gently mix the strips with two-thirds of the tomato sauce in a large bowl. Spread half of the strips in the bottom of the baking dish and cover with all of the mozzarella. Top with the remaining crêpe strips. Pour the rest of the sauce on top and then sprinkle with the Parmesan. Bake until the sauce is bubbling and the Parmesan is starting to brown, about 20 minutes. Let stand for 10 minutes. Serve with extra Parmesan on the side.

— Serves 6

Until a few years ago you couldn't find the ring-shaped pasta known as anelletti outside of Sicily, and I remember friends packing it in their suitcases to carry back to Rome or Milan to keep in their pantries for *timballo,* which, like *pasta con le sarde,* is one of our island's signature dishes. Sicilian families often take *timballo di anelletti* with them for picnics on the beach or for Pasquetta, the day after Easter. Because anelletti is a very hard pasta, it is almost impossible to overcook; once you've boiled the pasta and seasoned it with tomato sauce, you can bake the *timballo* for half an hour and the anelletti will still be nice and firm.

When I am feeling very decadent, I make a ragù of *stigghiole* to go with the anelletti. *Stigghiole*—a length of lamb intestine wrapped around onions and parsley and sometimes pecorino—is what I call a "hardcore delight," one that only a few family members go crazy for. The ragù is a sumptuous combination of fat and thick tomato paste, but certainly not something you could eat every day. Usually at Case Vecchie, I serve anelletti much more simply. Seasoned with our homemade tomato sauce and spoonfuls of fresh, creamy ricotta, it is beautiful to look at and lovely to eat!

Anelletti con Salsa Pronta e Ricotta
Anelletti with Tomato Sauce and Ricotta

12 ounces anelletti

2 cups Salsa Pronta (page 163) or good-quality tomato sauce

1½ cups whole-milk ricotta, preferably sheep's milk, divided

2 heaping tablespoons grated Parmesan, plus more for topping

Cook the anelletti in a large pot of boiling well-salted water.

Meanwhile, gently warm the tomato sauce in a small saucepan.

In a large serving bowl, mix 1 cup ricotta with a small ladle of pasta cooking water to create a stiff sauce. Drain the cooked pasta and add to the bowl, along with the tomato sauce. Top with the remaining ½ cup ricotta and sprinkle with the Parmesan. Serve hot.

— Serves 4 to 6

The salad tomatoes we grow are totally different from the tomatoes we use for sauce. Regaleali's huge beefsteaks have always been a dream. My grandmother was very keen on them, but no one knows where she first found the seeds. My mother also joined the tomato fan club and regularly brought back new seeds from the U.S. Case Grandi's tomatoes were pulpy and very sweet, while the ones from Case Vecchie were smaller and decidedly more acidic. I have also become a seed collector and have introduced yellow, green, and striped heirloom varieties from the U.S., which grow amazingly well in our soil. I tried hard to label and organize the different seeds, but between Carmelo at Case Grandi and Giovanni at Case Vecchie, everything has gotten mixed up, and we're never quite sure what will appear on the vines. Fortunately, it is a very delicious sort of surprise.

Call us fussy, but we always peel the tomatoes with a sharp knife when we make tomato salad. It makes them much more enjoyable to eat. Then we arrange them on one of our family platters with slices of red onion and a big pinch of dried oregano. Although I plant several different kinds of onions, we mostly use red onions in our kitchen. Tropea onions grow especially well in our soil, and I find them much more flavorful than the white or yellow ones and sweet enough to eat raw. Combining the purple ribbons of onion with the green, yellow, pink, and red tomatoes makes an especially beautiful salad.

Insalata di Pomodoro e Cipolle
Tomato and Onion Salad

1½ pounds tomatoes, peeled, cored, and cut into wedges

1 small red onion, preferably Tropea, halved lengthwise and thinly sliced

¼ cup extra-virgin olive oil

1 tablespoon red wine vinegar

1 tablespoon dried oregano, preferably wild

Fine sea salt

Gently combine the tomatoes and onion with the oil, vinegar, oregano, and salt to taste.

— Serves 4

My paternal grandmother, Conchita, was from a Spanish family that settled in Cuba, but she was brought up in England and spent most of her life between Rome and Paris. Now and then, a touch of "Cubo-Spanish" flavor pops up in the cuisine of that side of the family, such as the sliced bananas arranged around rice pilaf or a very glamorous gazpacho that my mother learned to make from her in-laws (though definitely not from my grandmother, who probably didn't even know where the kitchen was . . . at least that was the story my mother liked to tell). Years later, thanks to my Spanish friend Isabel Labayen, I discovered that our gazpacho, which was liquidy, very sweet, and loaded with basil, had nothing to do with the gazpacho you find in Spain. Nevertheless, my mother was very proud of her soup, and it was indeed delicious. Over the years, I developed my own gazpacho, which combines my mother's recipe with a few tips from Isabel. The flavor is more traditionally Spanish, but I still pass the soup through a sieve like my mother did, so its consistency is hers.

Gazpacho
Chilled Tomato Soup

2 pounds tomatoes, cored and
   quartered

1 cucumber, peeled and coarsely
   chopped

1 red bell pepper, coarsely chopped

1 red onion, coarsely chopped

¼ cup red or white wine vinegar,
   or to taste

¼ cup extra-virgin olive oil

Fine sea salt

Put the tomatoes in a blender and blend on high until very smooth. Add the cucumber, bell pepper, and onion in batches and blend together until very smooth. Stir in the vinegar, oil, and salt to taste. Taste and adjust the seasoning to your preferences. Pour the gazpacho through a fine-mesh sieve into a large bowl, pressing on and discarding any solids.

Refrigerate the gazpacho until very cold. I like to serve this with toasted bread.

— Serves 4 to 6

Enza just might be the sweetest person in the whole world. She has lived in Vallelunga her whole life and is married to one of Giovanna's brothers; together, they have two sons. Her father keeps cows in the hills above the village, and a few years ago somebody stole the whole herd during the night. We were all shocked—how could thirty cows disappear without a trace? It is still a mystery.

If Giovanna is my right arm, Enza is my left. She has a special gift for pastry, and every year for the feast of San Giuseppe, she is in charge of preparing the little sponge cake swans covered with a thick yellow cream for the village feast. Enza brings her smile into the kitchen every morning—she is indispensable in keeping up the group's good mood!

As with tomato sauce, many Sicilian housekeepers still make their own *estratto*. Even in Palermo, among the chaos of cars, noise, and smog, you will see roof terraces dotted with tables of tomato paste drying in the August sun. I can't think of anything more quintessentially Sicilian than *estratto*; its intense, almost sunburnt taste is unique. When it is freshly made, Giovanna and I have a hard time resisting it, and I often like to have it on my toast at breakfast! But usually we use *estratto* to flavor vegetable soups and meat-based dishes; it enriches both the flavor and the body of a sauce. In fact, it is so dense that in most cases you must dissolve it in a glass of wine or water before adding it to the other ingredients.

I like to say that *estratto* is made of three basic ingredients: tomato, salt, and sun. My friend Martino Ragusa adds a fourth ingredient to the list: patience. First, we must predict when the warmest, driest days of the year will occur and before then order in huge quantities of tomatoes. As with the *salsa pronta*, the tomatoes are boiled in giant pots and then ground to a bright red puree, which is spread on wooden tables in the courtyard to dry in the sun. Over a day or two, the puree thickens into a very dark red paste with the consistency of clay. We stir the puree every half hour (Martino recommends every ten minutes!) to prevent a crust from forming, and at night we carry the boards into a storeroom so dew can't gather on the paste during the night. Patience is indeed key to the whole endeavor, but there is a kind of euphoria that overtakes us as the sun beats down on our heads and we dance around those tables covered with red goop!

Because so much is left to timing, the sun, and the quality of the tomatoes, I can only offer a rough outline for how to make *estratto*, not an exact recipe. Keep in mind that during the drying process the fresh tomatoes should reduce down to about a tenth of their initial weight; for example, if we want to wind up with twenty pounds of *estratto*, we will start with about two hundred pounds of tomatoes.

To begin, cook whole Roma tomatoes with plenty of garlic, red onion, fresh bay leaves, and salt. When the tomatoes have broken down into a rough puree, pass them through a food mill to remove the skin and seeds. Taste the puree and season with salt to taste, then pour the puree directly onto a large unfinished wooden board or tabletop in the sun and begin to stir it with your hands or a spoon.

The puree has to be spread out, gathered in, stirred, and spread out again frequently so that the sun can evaporate the water. Overnight, put the table on a porch or a place where it will have fresh air but moisture cannot collect on it. If the sun is not very hot, the drying process may take two days or more.

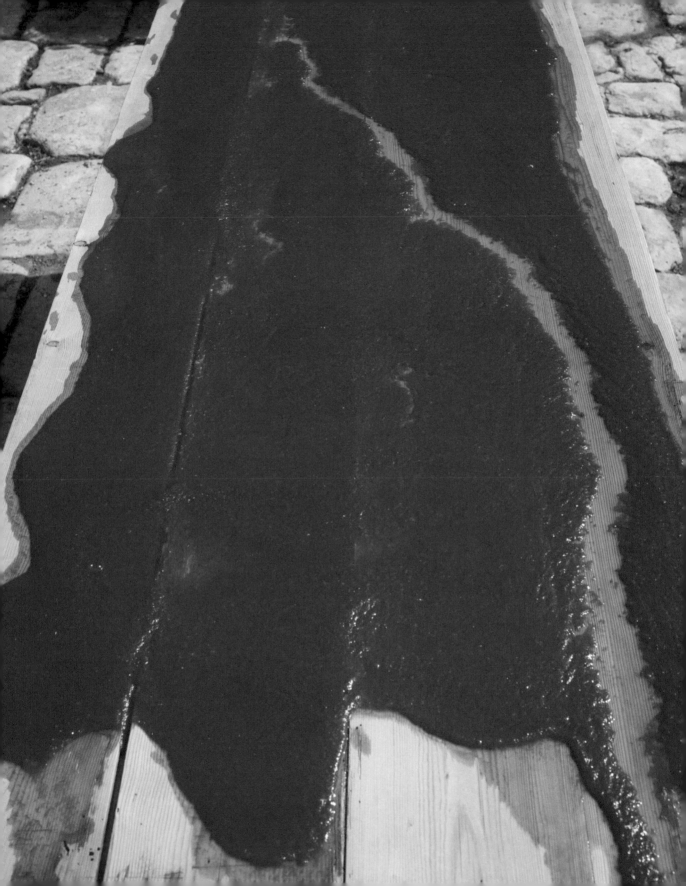

When the *estratto* has become so thick that it can be molded like clay, oil your hands well and pack the paste little by little into sterilized glass jars, pressing down well so that no air bubbles remain. Coat the surface with a thin layer of oil, cover tightly, and store in a cool, dark place. Each time you take some paste out, make sure that the remaining surface is covered with oil. Stored this way, *estratto* will keep for up to a year in the refrigerator.

You will see *estratto* called for throughout the book in recipes like Arancine (page 284) and Tuna Ragù (page 136). It is also used in the following recipe, which I learned from Giuseppe, a sailor who works at our family's sailing club in Mondello. Tiny octopuses are rare, even in Sicily, so it is cause for celebration when we find them at the market. *Murati* means "walled," and these octopuses are stewed gently in a lidded clay pot with some onion, *estratto*, and wine until very tender.

Polipetti Murati
Slow-Cooked Octopus with Estratto and Wine

½ cup extra-virgin olive oil

1 large red onion, finely chopped

1 or 2 garlic cloves, peeled and smashed

2 pounds small octopuses (the smaller the better)

1 cup white wine, divided

Red pepper flakes

1 tablespoon *estratto* or other good quality sun-dried tomato paste

Fine sea salt

Combine the olive oil, onion, and garlic in a medium pot, preferably earthenware (stovetop safe), and cook over medium-high heat until the onion and garlic are golden, about 5 minutes. Remove the garlic and discard it. Add the octopuses and cook 5 minutes. Add ½ cup wine and the red pepper flakes to taste, and cook until the wine has evaporated.

Meanwhile, dissolve the *estratto* in the remaining ½ cup wine. Add to the octopuses, stirring well. If the mixture looks too dry, add ½ cup water. Bring to a boil, then reduce the heat to low, cover, and cook until the octopus is very tender and the sauce has thickened, 20 to 30 minutes. Season with salt to taste.

— Serves 6 to 8

My mother discovered this dish in Pantelleria, which is why she called it *pasta all'isolana*. As I've said before, Pantelleria's rich volcanic soil produces the most intensely flavored vegetables, and tomatoes are no exception. I have often brought seeds from there or the Aeolian Islands to plant in Case Vecchie's garden, and though they turn out well, they are still missing that certain combination of mineral tang, salt, and sweetness. For this recipe, make sure you use the best sun-dried tomatoes you can find; they should be tender and pliable and rich in flavor, not tasting of *cauciù* (leather)!

Pasta all'Isolana
Pasta with Cherry Tomatoes and Sun-Dried Tomatoes

4 ounces good-quality sun-dried tomatoes

½ cup extra-virgin olive oil

2 garlic cloves, peeled

8 ounces cherry tomatoes, halved or quartered depending on their size

Red pepper flakes

Fine sea salt

1 pound spaghetti

1 small bunch fresh basil

Puree the sun-dried tomatoes in a blender or food processor until smooth. Set aside. Combine the olive oil and garlic in a small saucepan and cook over medium heat, until the garlic is golden and the oil is fragrant, about 3 minutes. Remove from the heat and discard the garlic. Gently stir together the cherry tomatoes, pureed sun-dried tomatoes, and garlic oil on a large serving platter. Season with red pepper flakes and salt to taste.

Meanwhile, cook the spaghetti in a large pot of boiling well-salted water. Drain and gently mix the spaghetti with the tomato mixture. Tear basil leaves over the pasta and serve hot.

— *Serves 4*

EGGPLANT

Eggplants are to Sicilians what potatoes are to the Irish. So many types of eggplants are grown here—the long black ones that are perfect for caponata, the spherical purple *tunisine* eggplants that originally came from Tunisia and are so good *alla parmigiana*, and the miniature purple *perlina*—and we use them all. Because we do eat so many of them, it's funny to note that the word for eggplant, *melanzana*, translates to "insane apple"—*mela non sana*—since it resembles an apple but can't be eaten raw (like any member of the nightshade family, it contains some toxic substances). Together, eggplants and tomatoes are a vital part of our summer landscape. You see them everywhere, growing in gardens and piled high in the backs of green grocer trucks that travel from town to town.

Caponata is another cornerstone of Sicilian cuisine, and everyone who tastes my version loves it. It is delicious as a side dish with fish or meat, but I also like to serve it with cheese, especially Formaggio all'Argentiera (page 59). Caponata tastes best if made ahead, but each ingredient should still be distinct. Keeping the cooking time to a minimum helps retain a light, fresh feeling that is not often associated with this dish.

Caponata di Melanzana
Eggplant Caponata

1 small bunch celery, tough outer stalks discarded, strings removed, and coarsely sliced

Vegetable oil, for frying

2 pounds eggplant, cut into 1-inch cubes

Fine sea salt

¼ cup extra-virgin olive oil

1 large red onion, halved lengthwise and thinly sliced

1 cup green olives, pitted and cut lengthwise into thirds

¼ cup capers, rinsed and drained

1½ cups Salsa Pronta (page 163) or good-quality tomato sauce

¼ cup red or white wine vinegar

1 tablespoon sugar, or to taste

5 hard-boiled eggs, peeled and quartered lengthwise, for garnish

¼ cup chopped fresh flat-leaf parsley, for garnish

Cook the celery in a small pot of boiling water until crisp-tender, about 5 minutes. Drain and rinse under cold running water until cooled. Drain well and set aside.

Heat 1 inch of vegetable oil in a large heavy skillet. Add the eggplant in batches and fry until well browned all over, about 5 minutes. Drain on paper towels. Season with salt.

Combine the olive oil and onion in a large skillet and cook over medium-high heat until just golden, about 5 minutes. Add the reserved celery, olives, capers, tomato sauce, vinegar, sugar, and salt to taste. Gently stir in the eggplant, being careful not to break up the pieces. Simmer for 2 to 3 minutes, then transfer to a large bowl or platter and cool.

Garnish the caponata with the hard-boiled eggs and chopped parsley, and serve cold or at room temperature.

— Serves 8 to 10

I often prepare eggplant involtini in the summer—the way the dish blends the sweetness of fried eggplant with the sweetness of our tomato sauce has made it a favorite of our guests. I think of it as a much more casual version of an eggplant and pasta *timballo*, a celebrated *monsù* recipe, but I daresay it is even more delicious.

Involtini di Melanzane
Eggplant Roll-Ups

Olive oil, for frying, plus more for the baking dish

4 or 5 large eggplants, cut lengthwise into ½-inch-thick slices

10 ounces capellini or angel hair pasta

8 cups Salsa Pronta (page 163) or good-quality tomato sauce, divided

⅓ cup finely grated Parmesan, plus more for sprinkling

1 large sprig fresh basil, mint, or oregano

Heat 1½ inches of olive oil in a large heavy skillet. Add the eggplant slices in batches and fry, flipping halfway through, until deep golden brown, 5 to 7 minutes. Drain on paper towels.

Meanwhile, cook the pasta in a large pot of boiling well-salted water for 1 minute (pasta must be almost crunchy when you take it out because it will cook further in the oven). Drain well, then transfer to a large bowl and toss with 6 cups of the cold tomato sauce and ⅓ cup Parmesan.

Preheat the oven to 350°F. Drizzle the bottom of a large ceramic baking dish with olive oil and cover with 1 cup tomato sauce.

Put 1 eggplant slice on a work surface and place a small handful of pasta in the middle and roll up. Place in the baking dish and repeat with the remaining eggplant slices and pasta, packing the rolls snugly into the dish. Cover with the remaining tomato sauce and sprinkle with some Parmesan. Tuck a few leaves of fresh herbs between the rolls. Bake until the cheese is melted and the sauce is bubbling, 20 to 25 minutes.

— *Serves 10 (2 involtini per person)*

The word *ammuttunate* in Sicilian means "closed but ready to open," like the bud of a rose. In the Palermitan version of this recipe, the eggplant is stuffed with caciocavallo, garlic, and basil and fried, then simmered in tomato sauce. I prefer Giovanna's recipe from Vallelunga, which is much simpler and omits the frying. The whole eggplant is first sautéed in olive oil with onion and garlic and then simmered in tomato sauce until tender.

A few years ago my mother started planting *perlina*—miniature eggplants grown in the area of Comiso, west of Ragusa—which seem like they would be perfect fried in a tempura batter. I tried, but they never cooked fully by the time the batter was golden. But they do work beautifully in the *ammuttunate*.

Melanzane Ammuttunate
Whole Eggplants Stewed in Tomato Sauce

⅓ cup extra-virgin olive oil

1 small red onion, chopped

1 garlic clove, finely chopped

2 large eggplants or 12 very small eggplants (perlina or Fairy Tale), stems trimmed

Fine sea salt and black pepper

1 cup Salsa Pronta (page 163) or good-quality tomato sauce

4 ounces pecorino, coarsely chopped (optional)

Combine the olive oil, onion, and garlic in a large saucepan and cook over medium heat until the onion is softened, about 5 minutes. Add the whole eggplants and cook until the skins change color, about 5 minutes. Season with salt and pepper, then add the tomato sauce. Reduce the heat and cook, covered, stirring occasionally to keep the bottom from sticking, until the eggplants are tender, 15 to 20 minutes. Add the pecorino (if using) and cook, uncovered, about 5 minutes. Serve warm.

— Serves 4 as a side dish

An infinite number of recipes exist for the vegetarian stew known as *canazzo*: Agostina, my family's housekeeper in Mondello, used to fry the eggplants separately and add them at the end. Michela, my current housekeeper in Palermo, adds vinegar and sugar for a sweet and sour flavor. I like Giovanna's version best because it is so easy to make and comforting to eat. She introduces all the ingredients at once and plays with the lid to make sure that potatoes and eggplants get cooked at the same time.

Canazzo di Giovanna
Giovanna's Vegetable Stew

⅔ cup extra-virgin olive oil

4 potatoes, peeled and chopped into 1-inch chunks

2 red bell peppers, chopped into 2-inch pieces

2 red onions, halved lengthwise and cut into 1-inch-thick slices

1 large eggplant, cut into 2-inch cubes

1 cup canned Roma (plum) tomatoes, chopped

1 tablespoon dried oregano, preferably wild

2 teaspoons fine sea salt

½ teaspoon black pepper

Combine the olive oil, potatoes, bell peppers, onions, and eggplant in a very large skillet and cook over medium heat, stirring, until everything is well coated with oil, 5 to 7 minutes. Stir in the tomatoes, oregano, salt, and black pepper, then reduce to a simmer, and cook, covered, until the vegetables are tender, about 30 minutes.

— Serves 6 to 8

When I was an art historian and museum curator

in Veneto, my assistant, Romina, arrived one day with a small bottle of elderflower syrup, not knowing that she was about to change our lives. Mixed with ice water and a drop of lemon juice, this syrup makes the freshest, most incredible drink—it's like drinking flowers!—and we now always serve it to guests at the start of a cooking lesson. The elderberry tree is ubiquitous and grows like a weed in both the north and south of Italy, but its blossoms are not commonly used in Sicily. My friend Rachel Lam, who is a gardener in Sicily but originally comes from England, tells me that there they make a fizzy summer drink with the syrup, which they call elderflower champagne. We pick the airy blossoms when they are pale yellow and very fragrant, and then it is short work to make this syrup.

Sambuca
Elderflower Syrup

1½ lemons

5 pounds sugar

10 cups water

15 elderflower blossoms

With a peeler or a sharp knife, cut the zest off the lemons. Juice the lemons and set aside.

Combine the sugar, water, and lemon zest in a large pot and cook, stirring, over medium-high heat until the sugar is dissolved and the mixture is syrupy. Remove from the heat and cool until tepid.

Stir in the elderflower blossoms and the reserved lemon juice. Let stand for 24 hours, then pour through a fine-mesh sieve into bottles or jars and seal tightly.

To serve, fill a pitcher with ice water and stir in a squeeze of lemon juice and elderflower syrup to taste. Serve over ice.

— Makes 8 quarts

ZUCCHINI

I met my dear friend Niloufer Ichaporia King, the cookbook author, over a zucchini recipe. I had just given a talk at the Italian Cultural Institute of San Francisco, and Niloufer, nibbling a piece of *sfincione* I had made, approached me with a question about the soup that Sicilians make with *cucuzze*. She was familiar with this very long, pale green zucchini because it is also used in India. I don't think it's an accident that our friendship started over such an unpretentious recipe. Although we come from different cultures, our feelings about food are as one, and we both use cooking as a way to express our affection and sympathy.

That is the reason I like to offer this soup to jet-lagged guests. In terms of love and comfort, Zucchini Soup with Tender Greens in the summer is the equivalent of Capellini in Chicken Broth with Ricotta (page 55) in the winter. *Tenerumi* are the floppy leaves and tendrils of the *cucuzze* plant; they have a sweet, delicate taste. At markets in Sicily you will often find them for sale in bundles next to the *cucuzze*.

Minestra di Tenerumi e Cucuzze
Zucchini Soup with Tender Greens

½ cup extra-virgin olive oil

1 red onion, chopped

2 garlic cloves, chopped

2 tomatoes, peeled and chopped, or 1½ cups canned Roma (plum) tomatoes, chopped

Fine sea salt and black pepper

2 *cucuzze* squash or 3 medium zucchini, peeled and chopped

3 bunches *tenerumi* or tender squash greens, chopped

1 small bunch celery leaves, chopped

3 small potatoes, peeled and chopped

4 cups lukewarm water

Combine the olive oil, onion, and garlic in a large, wide soup pot and cook over medium-high heat until the onion is golden, about 5 minutes. Add the tomatoes and cook, breaking them up with a wooden spoon, 2 to 3 minutes. Season with salt and pepper. Add the rest of the vegetables and simmer 2 minutes. Add the water, then simmer, covered, until the vegetables are tender, 20 to 25 minutes.

— Serves 6 to 8

When I was living in Verona and returned to Sicily for the summer holidays, Mario always prepared Zucchini Soup with Tender Greens for me, as well as an incredibly comforting stew of *cucuzze* and tomato sauce—these were the two dishes that meant I was home.

Zucchine a Spezzatino
Zucchini Stewed in Tomato Sauce

¼ cup extra-virgin olive oil

1 large onion, chopped

1 *cucuzze* squash or 2 medium zucchini, peeled and coarsely chopped

1 teaspoon fine sea salt

1 cup Salsa Pronta (page 163) or good-quality tomato sauce

2 tablespoons chopped fresh basil

Finely grated Parmesan, for serving

Combine the olive oil and onion in a large saucepan and cook over medium heat until softened, about 5 minutes. Add the squash and salt and cook, stirring to coat in oil, about 2 minutes. Stir in the tomato sauce, then reduce the heat to low and cook, covered, until the squash is tender, 15 to 20 minutes. Remove from the heat and stir in the basil. Serve with the grated Parmesan.

— Serves 4

In August and September, we harvest the yellow blossoms from every kind of zucchini planted in the garden. We cook the blossoms in many different ways, but I like the following two recipes best. The linguine lets you really taste the sweetness of the blossoms, while the fried blossoms pair that sweetness with the salty tang of anchovies and cheese.

Linguine con Fiori di Zucca
Linguine with Squash Blossoms

½ cup extra-virgin olive oil

1 medium red onion, chopped

1 garlic clove, finely chopped

5 ounces (about 50) squash
    blossoms, stems removed

1 large tomato, peeled and chopped

½ cup white wine

Fine sea salt and black pepper

12 ounces spaghetti

Finely grated ricotta salata or
    Parmesan, for serving

Combine the olive oil, onion, and garlic in a large skillet and cook over medium heat until the onion is softened, about 5 minutes. Add the squash blossoms and cook, stirring gently, until wilted, about 3 minutes. Add the chopped tomato, bring to a boil, and cook 5 minutes. Stir in the wine and cook 5 minutes more. Season with salt and pepper to taste and continue to simmer until the blossoms are tender, about 5 minutes more.

Meanwhile, cook the spaghetti in a large pot of boiling well-salted water. Reserve a cup or so of the cooking water, then drain well. Toss the pasta and sauce together, adding some of the reserved pasta water if the dish looks dry. Sprinkle with plenty of cheese.

— Serves 4 to 6

Fiori di Zucca Fritti Ripieni
Stuffed Fried Squash Blossoms

12 squash blossoms

3 ounces provolone or mozzarella, cut into 12 pieces (about 2 inches long by ½ inch wide)

6 oil-packed anchovy fillets, halved

1⅓ cups durum wheat or semolina flour

1 (12-ounce) bottle ice-cold beer or fizzy mineral water

Fine sea salt and black pepper

Vegetable oil, for frying

Carefully stuff each squash blossom with 1 piece of provolone and 1 piece of anchovy. Stir together the flour and beer in a bowl until well combined (it should be quite dense, like a pancake batter). Season with salt and pepper to taste. Holding the blossoms by their stems, dip into the batter, twisting gently as you pull them out. Heat 1½ inches of oil in a large heavy skillet. Add the blossoms in batches, and fry, flipping halfway through, until puffed and golden brown, about 3 minutes. Drain on paper towels. Sprinkle with salt and serve warm.

— *Serves 4 to 6*

Pompeo, Giovanna's husband, looks after the courtyard at Case Vecchie. He is a big man, with a large, friendly face, though he rarely looks you straight in the eye. Pompeo loves chile peppers and dahlias, and I think that secretly he is also a good cook, since he was the one who taught me the wonderful Blood Orange Salad with Red Onion and Black Olives (page 25). He comes from a family of bakers, and we still buy our bread from his sister Franca, in Vallelunga. I have to admit I get a little anxious when I watch him pruning the jasmines or geraniums with his huge hands, but in fact he is very gentle with flowers. He also has a true passion for animals and cares for a number of cats—which my dog, Monsù, loves to chase—and one beautiful Maremma sheepdog, named Asia. During my first few years at Case Vecchie, Pompeo was also looking after the vegetable garden. He is at least as stubborn as I am, and I can't say we didn't argue over how things should be planted and cared for. But I was quite astonished when he, rather poetically, told me about the "eggs" of the artichokes, and I didn't dare contradict. I later discovered that is what people in Vallelunga call the little plants that shoot out from the main bush.

SWORDFISH

In Sicily, fresh fish has historically been the provenance of the wealthy; poorer people made do with preserved fish, usually salted or canned. On the flip side, going out to sea to fish is much more dangerous than working the land, and you need money to be well equipped. Until a few decades ago, tuna fisherman used a complex strategy called *mattanza* to lure a big bunch of tuna close to the coast, but it involved large groups of people and much of the work took place in very shallow water. But the hunt for swordfish belongs to the "real" fishing world. The channel between Messina and Reggio Calabria is Sicily's best-known hunting ground for swordfish, and fishermen are said to sing an ancient Greek song to enchant the fish and make the fishing easier.

Only in Palermo will you find *ruota di pesce spada*, a whole wheel—or thick cross-section—of swordfish stuffed with herbs and baked. I often buy this giant piece of fish from my friend Andrea at the Vucciria market, where I know it will be very fresh. It is an impressive and beautiful dish, but quite easy to prepare.

Ruota di Pesce Spada
Mint and Garlic–Stuffed Swordfish

6 garlic cloves, chopped

Leaves of 1 large bunch fresh mint

Coarse sea salt

1 (3-pound) center-cut piece of swordfish, about 5 inches thick

¾ cup extra-virgin olive oil

1 cup white wine

Preheat the oven to 400°F. Chop the garlic, mint, and salt together to make a rough paste. With a sharp knife, make 2-inch-deep slits in the flesh of the swordfish (both top and bottom) and stuff with the garlic-mint mixture, rubbing any extra on the outside of the fish. Drizzle the bottom of a shallow baking pan with some of the olive oil, put the fish in the pan, and drizzle with the remaining oil. Bake for 15 minutes, then pour the white wine over the fish. Reduce the temperature to 350°F and bake until opaque (check with the tip of a sharp knife), about 15 minutes more. Remove from the oven, loosely cover with foil, and let stand 10 minutes before serving.

— Serves 8

Marinating fish in olive oil, then dipping it in breadcrumbs and grilling it, is an easy method that produces a delicious result. I use this technique interchangeably with both swordfish and tuna steaks.

Pesce Spada Impanato
Grilled Swordfish Steaks with Breadcrumbs

1½ pounds swordfish or tuna steaks, about ¾ inch thick

⅔ cup extra-virgin olive oil

2 garlic cloves, peeled and smashed

1 teaspoon fine sea salt

½ teaspoon red pepper flakes

½ teaspoon black pepper

3 cups unseasoned dried breadcrumbs

Lemon wedges, for serving

Prepare a grill for cooking over medium-high heat (alternatively, use a grill pan on the stove).

Place the fish steaks in a deep pan and cover with the olive oil, garlic, salt, red pepper flakes, and black pepper, turning the fish to coat evenly. Marinate at room temperature for 30 minutes. Fill another dish with the breadcrumbs. Remove the steaks from the oil, then dredge in the breadcrumbs until thickly coated. Grill over medium-high heat until the breadcrumbs are deep golden-brown and the fish is cooked through, 3 to 4 minutes per side. Serve with lemon wedges.

— Serves 6

Swordfish involtini elaborates on the idea of *impanato*, first stuffing the swordfish pieces with a very Sicilian combination of breadcrumbs, currants, and pine nuts, and then dredging them in more breadcrumbs and baking them with bay leaves and orange and lemon slices. It's similar to the technique we use for the Involtini di Carne (page 290), but lighter and more summery.

Involtini di Pesce Spada
Swordfish Roll-Ups with Pine Nuts and Currants

¼ cup extra-virgin olive oil, plus more for coating

1 small red onion, finely chopped

2¾ cups unseasoned dried breadcrumbs, divided

1 lemon, half juiced, half thinly sliced

1 orange, half juiced, half thinly sliced

1 tablespoon dried currants

1 tablespoon pine nuts

⅓ cup chopped fresh mint

Fine sea salt and black pepper

1 pound swordfish, sliced into 8 thin pieces (about ⅓ inch thick; if the pieces are too thick, you can pound them gently between pieces of wax paper)

12 bay leaves, preferably fresh

Preheat the oven to 350°F. Drizzle the bottom of a medium baking dish with olive oil.

Combine the ¼ cup olive oil and onion in a medium skillet and cook over medium-high heat until softened, about 3 minutes. Remove from the heat and stir in ¾ cup breadcrumbs, mixing everything together until the breadcrumbs have absorbed the oil. Return to low heat and toast the breadcrumbs slightly. Remove from the heat and stir in the lemon and orange juices, the currants, pine nuts, and mint. Season with salt and pepper to taste.

Lay a piece of swordfish on a work surface and put a heaping tablespoon of the breadcrumb filling (squeeze it in your hand to compact it) in the center and roll up. Repeat with the remaining swordfish and filling.

Pour some olive oil into a shallow pan and fill another shallow pan with the remaining 2 cups breadcrumbs. Dip each roll-up first in the oil then dredge in the breadcrumbs until lightly coated. Place the swordfish roll-ups snugly in the baking dish and tuck the bay leaves and lemon and orange slices between the rolls. Drizzle with some more olive oil and bake until the fish is cooked through, about 10 minutes.

— Serves 4

SUMMERTIME DESSERTS

August is the month of figs, and you will see vendors selling them everywhere: in the markets, along the side of the highway, and from the backs of their old three-wheeled Apes. At Case Vecchie we grow both black and green figs, which we must protect from the birds by covering the trees with large white nets. Thus draped, the trees look beautiful and quite surreal, like ladies wrapped in turbans at the hairdresser; but this is the only way to keep the birds away. A friend told me that he once had a problem with magpies eating his peaches, and when he put up a net one of the birds got stuck and died. His gardener told him that if he hung the dead bird from one of his peach trees no other bird would dare pick the fruit. That may be so, but I don't think I can hang a sparrow to save my figs. I just hope there will be enough for everyone!

In my opinion, fig sorbet is the best sorbet we make at Case Vecchie. Our figs are so sweet that we need to add very little sugar, and they churn up into an incredible creaminess.

Sorbetto di Fichi
Fig Sorbet

1½ pounds fresh figs, peeled and halved

¾ cup sugar

Juice of ½ lemon

Freshly whipped cream, for serving

Combine the figs, sugar, and lemon juice in a blender and puree until very smooth. Refrigerate the mixture until very cold. Freeze the mixture in an ice cream maker, then transfer to an airtight container and put in the freezer to firm up. Serve with whipped cream.

— Makes about 1½ pints

Every country has its own way of pruning trees. Here, we tend to open the tree in the shape of a chandelier, with four or five main arms set in opposite directions. They are never allowed to grow too high, which makes it easier to collect the fruit and protects them from the harsh north winds. The mulberry tree my mother planted in the garden of Case Vecchie is now about twenty years old, and I am happy to have inherited this gorgeous round cupola. In the summer, you need to bend a little to get under the tree, and when you straighten up, you find yourself sheltered inside a beautiful dome dotted with black and red fruits. Mulberry trees were once common in this area because the fruit was used to feed silkworms. Now you often find mulberry trees abandoned in the countryside, overgrown and full of berries that, sadly, no one collects. One of the best ways to appreciate this berry is in sorbet, which is sweet, tart, and refreshing.

Sorbetto di Gelsi Neri
Mulberry Sorbet

5 cups mulberries   1 cup sugar

Combine the mulberries and sugar in a blender and puree until very smooth. Pour through a fine-mesh sieve into a medium bowl and refrigerate the mixture until very cold. Freeze in an ice cream maker, then transfer to an airtight container and put in the freezer to firm up.

— *Makes about 1½ pints*

Amarene incileppate are sour cherries cooked in sugar syrup and served very cold, almost like a sort of sorbet. I would go crazy for them when I had them at my grandparents' table. These days, I gather all the ripe sour cherries I can get hold of, then cook and freeze them in so I can eat them all year long.

Amarene Incileppate
Sour Cherries in Sugar Syrup

2 pounds sour cherries (about
  5 cups), pitted

2¼ cups sugar

Combine the cherries and sugar in a large pot and cook over medium heat, stirring, until the sugar is dissolved, about 5 minutes. Remove from the heat, then cool completely. Serve or freeze for later use.

— Makes about 6 cups

Coffee is a staple in Sicily. "Real" men prefer the dark, creamy, and very tiny espressos you sip while standing up at the bar. Women make coffee at home with the silver stovetop moka pot. I think of coffee pudding as a feminine version of the topic, sweet and very fragrant. Be careful to use decaffeinated coffee for this, otherwise no one will sleep afterward!

Gelo di Caffé
Coffee Pudding

¾ cup instant coffee granules,
  preferably decaffeinated

4 cups lukewarm water

1⅓ cups sugar

¾ cup cornstarch or wheat starch

Finely grated zest of 1 lemon

Lightly sweetened whipped cream,
  for serving

Combine the coffee and water in a medium saucepan and stir until the coffee is dissolved. Add the sugar, cornstarch, and lemon zest and cook over medium-low heat, stirring constantly, until the mixture thickens, about 20 minutes. When it comes to a boil, cook 1 minute more, then remove from the heat and pour through a fine-mesh sieve into a medium bowl. Refrigerate until very cold and firm. Before serving, unmold onto a serving platter and serve with the whipped cream.

— Serves 8

One summer I was vacationing on the island of Alicudi and had invited my friend Stefania Barzini, an excellent cook and renowned cookbook author, to dinner. I knew she had a soft spot for watermelon pudding, which we call *gelo di mellone*, and I wanted to make it for her. But there was a problem. Alicudi is the most primitive of the Aeolian Islands—no cars are allowed, the houses are perched high up on the hills, and you measure where your house is by the number of steps you must climb from the sea—and my house was at four hundred steps. There was no way I could carry a watermelon that far on my back. So I had to hire a donkey to bring a twenty-five-pound watermelon up to my house! Fortunately, the melon made the journey safely, and Stefania loved the pudding. When I make the pudding at Case Vecchie, I like to pick a few jasmine blossoms from the vines that grow in the courtyard for decoration; shavings of bittersweet chocolate also make a nice garnish.

Gelo di Mellone
Watermelon Pudding

1 (7-pound) watermelon

1 scant cup cornstarch or wheat starch

1 cup sugar, or to taste, depending on the sweetness of the melon

Fresh jasmine blossoms, bittersweet chocolate shavings, candied squash, or chopped pistachios, for garnish

Coarsely chop the watermelon into chunks, discarding the rinds. Puree enough watermelon flesh in a blender to yield 6 cups. Strain the watermelon puree through a fine-mesh sieve into a medium saucepan. Whisk in the cornstarch and sugar and bring to a boil, whisking constantly to prevent lumps. When it comes to a boil, cook for 1 minute, then remove from the heat and pour into glasses. Cool, then refrigerate until cold. Before serving, garnish as desired.

— Serves 10 to 12

Mario used to bring *taralli* from Mistretta for my grandparents, and my grandfather especially loved dipping these crisp knots into coffee for breakfast. The cookies were always kept in tins in my grandparents' dining room, and I can clearly remember the scent of sugar and lemon when you entered that room. My mother rediscovered the recipe and started making them herself. They make a nice accompaniment to any kind of pudding or sorbet.

Taralli
Lemony Knotted Cookies

4 cups all-purpose flour

½ cup granulated sugar

½ cup lard

2 tablespoons powdered ammonium bicarbonate, also called hartshorn

Finely grated zest of 1 lemon, plus the juice of 1 to 2 lemons

Pinch of fine sea salt

2 eggs

⅔ cup whole milk, lukewarm

2 cups powdered sugar

Mix the flour and granulated sugar together on a work surface. With your hands, work in the lard, ammonium bicarbonate, lemon zest, and salt. Make a well in the center and start working in the eggs, and then the milk, bit by bit, with your hands, just until the mixture comes together into a very soft dough (you may not need to use all the milk). Knead the dough vigorously; it is done when the dough pulls off your fingers easily but is still sticky.

Preheat the oven to 350°F. Line two baking sheets with parchment paper.

On a lightly floured surface, roll a piece of dough into a ½-inch-thick rope; cut crosswise into 5-inch lengths. Shape each length of dough into a looped knot and place on the baking sheet. Repeat with the remaining dough. Bake until golden brown, about 20 minutes.

Meanwhile, in a small bowl, mix the powdered sugar and enough lemon juice to achieve a glaze consistency.

Dip the top of each cookie in the icing and transfer to a rack to cool.

— Makes about 4 dozen

FALL

By the first of September, the winery's doors are wide open, like huge mouths waiting to be fed by the grapes. The harvest is going at full speed, and the dirt road connecting Case Vecchie and Case Grandi is stained here and there with purple, mementos of grapes that have fallen off the truck on their way to the winery.

The smell of must is everywhere, and there is a sort of fizz in the air. Everyone rushes about, somewhat stressed but in many ways euphoric, especially when the weather stays clear.

It is quite a drama if the rains come during the harvest, and I remember my grandfather anxiously checking the sky several times a day. If the weather does turn bad, my cousin Alberto takes the huge portrait of my grandfather hanging in the living room of Case Grandi and sets it on an easel by the fire where we all think he is happier—a small superstitious gesture in the hopes that he will clear the weather.

When I was eighteen, I had some time on my hands before going to Aix-en-Provence to study classical Greek and Latin literature, a move that was probably generated more by my passionate devotion to my professor than passion for the subject (indeed, after a boring year of translations, I moved my concentration to art history). During this period, I decided to work at Regaleali for the grape harvest. At that time, Regaleali operated on a much smaller scale than it does today, with none of the twenty-first century's reliance on modern machinery or computerized systems. I remember men using pitchforks to move grapes into a huge hole where they would be crushed, a job that is now handled by conveyor belts.

My job was to record weights at the *bilico*, an enormous scale that weighed the trucks when they were loaded with grapes and again after they had dumped them out. First came the grapes from the estate and then the grapes from our neighbors, which we used to augment our own production (today, we use only our own grapes, from various properties throughout Sicily). Most of those grape sellers came from Valledolmo, and they dressed carefully for the occasion—moleskin or velvet trousers, sober shirts buttoned up to the chin, heavy shoes, and the traditional *coppola* hat. You could see by looking at their faces, which were strong, sunburnt, and crisscrossed with wrinkles, that they had personally cured their vines during the year to ensure a good harvest. I now feel privileged that I was able to get a glimpse of this little-known Sicily.

After work I used to eat dinner with my grandparents, then later my grandmother and I would go over my records, checking the weights and figures for each delivery of grapes. I must admit that my accounting was not always perfect, while my grandmother had a real flair for it. If things were really wrong, the next morning she would leave a loving note for me, inviting me to correct the numbers and to pay more attention the next time. I still keep those notes in my purse.

GRAPES AND VINO COTTO

Besides following the day-by-day grape harvest with curiosity and a little anxiety, at the school we take this moment to make grape crostata and vino cotto. For both we have always used the Inzolia grape, a small green, seedless variety that grows everywhere around Sicily. The fruits are perfectly round and sweet but still have a strong note of acidity. There are a few Inzolia vines planted just behind Case Vecchie, where we collect the grapes to make *crostata d'uva*. I once made this crostata using different grapes, ones that were sweeter but full of pits. It wasn't a success—people were spitting out the pits with each bite of cake! Since then, I stick to Inzolia or take the time to pit the grapes.

Crostata d'Uva
Grape Crostata

DOUGH

4¼ cups all-purpose flour

1 cup sugar

Pinch of fine sea salt

4 egg yolks, plus 1 whole egg

1¾ sticks (7 ounces) butter, at cool room temperature, cut into pieces

Whole milk, as needed

FILLING

½ cup Tangerine Marmalade (page 8) or good-quality store-bought marmalade

2 pounds small grapes, halved and pitted if necessary

2 tablespoons brown sugar

1 tablespoon butter, cut into pieces

Make the dough: Combine all the dough ingredients in the bowl of an electric mixer and mix together quickly until the dough just comes together. Do not overwork. If necessary, add a drop of milk. (If mixing by hand, mound the flour and make a well in the center. Add the sugar, salt, yolks, and whole egg to the well and mix in, little by little. Once it is all incorporated, make another well and add the butter in small pieces. Incorporate quickly.)

Preheat the oven to 350°F. Butter and flour a 10-inch springform pan.

On a floured work surface, roll out the dough into a ¼-inch-thick round. Fit the dough into the pan, then trim the edges so the sides are 1 inch high. (You can also pat the dough into the pan.)

Prepare the filling: Cover the bottom of the dough with the marmalade and then cover completely with grapes (pile them up because they will cook down). Sprinkle the brown sugar over the grapes and dot with the butter. Bake until the pastry is deep golden, 30 to 45 minutes.

Note: The recipe for Crostata d'Uva makes a generous amount of dough. I use the leftover dough to make biscotti regina, *a popular cookie that you will find in every* pasticceria *in Sicily. These tasty golden cookies are covered with sesame seeds and are very crunchy. To make them, preheat the oven to 350°F. Take the extra dough and roll it into a long, ¾- to 1-inch-thick rope. Cut the rope into 2-inch pieces. Fill a bowl with cold water and another with sesame seeds. Working in batches, quickly dip several pieces of dough in the water, then in the sesame seeds to coat. Arrange on a baking sheet and bake until golden brown, 20 to 30 minutes. Transfer to a rack to cool.*

— Serves 8 to 10

Every fall I call Laura Orsi, Regaleali's winemaker, to see when the Inzolia harvest is scheduled. When she gives me the word, I head up to the winery with an empty bucket and ask one of the men to fill it up from one of the huge pumps: In order to make vino cotto I need the must, or juice, pure, before anything has been added to it. Meanwhile, Pompeo and Salvatore have gone out into the fields to pick up some *sarmenti*, twisted twigs left over from pruning the vines, which they use to build a big fire in the courtyard at Case Vecchie. After the fire has burned down, the ashes are strained and kept in a bronze bucket. These powdery ashes will be used to purify the vino cotto and lessen the acidity of the grape juice.

To start, we have to boil the must for at least ten minutes to keep it from fermenting. Since it is still quite warm in September, the grape juice can ferment very quickly. Once it has cooled, we stir in the ashes—about four ounces of ashes per ten quarts of must—and let the whole thing sit for about twenty-four hours. After that time, the ashes should rise to the surface, clarifying the must. Then we strain the juice and start cooking it again, this time with orange zest, carob, cloves, bay leaves, and eventually some sugar, until it has reduced by half. The syrupy result has an incredibly rich flavor, the brightness of the grape juice deepened by nuances of caramel and spice.

Vino cotto was surely used before the arrival of sugarcane as a sweetener for many types of food and probably also to cover the gaminess of certain meats. While veal or lamb were reserved for special occasions, peasants got most of their meat by hunting, and vino cotto was perfect for softening game's wild flavor. I remember interviewing some old men from the Aeolian Islands who told stories of peasants who, spying the bumpy back of a tortoise on the surface of the calm winter sea, abandoned their jobs in the fields. They took their boats out, plucked the turtle, unaware, from the water and cooked it with lots of onions and vino cotto! It sounded more like an exotic Asian dish than something from the center of the Mediterranean.

We still use vino cotto in a few savory preparations with game or rabbit, but since today's meat lacks the past's wildness of flavor, you have to be careful not to add too much vino cotto to the dish and run the risk of turning it into a rabbit marmalade.

Coniglio al Vino Cotto
Pan-Roasted Rabbit with Vino Cotto

¾ cup extra-virgin olive oil

1 medium red onion, chopped

1 (3-pound) rabbit, cut into 8 pieces

Fine sea salt and black pepper

¾ cup vino cotto

3 sprigs fresh rosemary

1 cup warm water

Combine the olive oil and onion in a large skillet and cook over medium-high heat until golden, about 5 minutes. Add the rabbit and stir to coat with oil, then cook until well browned, 8 to 10 minutes. Season with salt and pepper to taste, then add the vino cotto and rosemary. Cook for about 5 minutes to reduce the vino cotto a bit. Add the warm water, reduce heat to low, and cook, covered, until the rabbit is tender and cooked through, about 30 minutes.

— *Serves 4 to 6*

Bavaroise was one of Mario's classic desserts, and he would often present two kinds—a dark one with cocoa and a white vanilla one—both dancing on the silver serving pieces that my grandmother used for big family dinners. I never considered bavaroise to be my soul dish (that place is forever reserved for chocolate profiteroles!), but those dancing towers were so beautiful I had to possess their secret. Over time, I made a few adjustments to Mario's recipe, adding some lemon zest and cinnamon to the custard and, as a final, absolutely divine touch, a drizzle of vino cotto.

Bavaroise al Vino Cotto
Bavaroise with Vino Cotto

4 cups whole milk

1 stick of cinnamon

Finely grated zest of 1 lemon

½ cup sugar

5 gelatin sheets

5 egg yolks

Vino cotto, for serving

Combine the milk, cinnamon, and lemon zest in a medium saucepan and heat over medium-low heat until warm. Add the sugar and gelatin and cook just until they are dissolved. Remove from the heat. Whisk together the egg yolks and then slowly whisk the yolks into the milk mixture until incorporated (be careful not to add too quickly or the eggs will cook). Pour the mixture through a fine-mesh sieve into a gelatin mold and chill until firm, at least 8 hours. When ready to serve, unmold and serve with vino cotto on the side.

— Serves 6 to 8

WILD GREENS

Wild greens start growing when the first big rains come after summer, usually around October and November. In the mountains and remote hills, where humans have neither planted nor pruned, the fields are left totally wild and become carpeted by all sorts of edible weeds, such as various field mustards that we call *mazzareddi*, *cavolicelli di vigna*, and *senapa*, as well as *sparacelli amari* (bitter cress), wild chicory, *cardedda* (sow thistle), and a kind of chard that we call *salachi*. Along the grapevines or on the edges of the seeded gardens, you will find purslane peeping out, which is excellent in salads, as well as mallow and wood sorrel, which, in Sicily, we call *agriduci* for its sweet and sour flavor.

When Carmelo or Salvatore heads out to pick a big bunch of *cavolicelli di vigna*, which often grows in the fields and among the grapevines, I know we are in for my kind of feast. It takes ages to pick and clean the greens, but their wild, fresh taste, enlivened in some cases by a kick of bitterness, makes them truly delicious.

My father, who was raised on French cuisine and prefers his spinach sautéed in butter, looks at these greens with disdain and declares them much too healthy for him. My mother and I were quite a different story, happily devouring a simple dish of spaghetti with sautéed *mazzareddi*. To this day, a plain platter of *salachi* seasoned with olive oil and lemon or sautéed with garlic and chile pepper is my idea of a perfect meal.

Verdure di Campo con Olio e Limone
Lemony Wild Greens

1½ pounds wild greens, chopped into 2-inch pieces (Swiss chard, kale, broccoli rabe, mustard greens, dandelion, spinach, arugula, and/or escarole can be substituted)

⅓ cup extra-virgin olive oil

Juice of 1 lemon

Fine sea salt

Cook the greens in a large pot of boiling well-salted water until they have lost some of their bitterness, about 10 minutes. Drain well, then mix the greens with the olive oil, lemon juice, and salt to taste. Serve warm or at room temperature.

— *Serves 4*

Verdura di Campo Saltata con Olio e Aglio
Wild Greens Sautéed with Olive Oil and Garlic

1½ pounds wild greens (Swiss chard, kale, broccoli rabe, mustard greens, dandelion, spinach, arugula, and/or escarole can be substituted)

¼ cup extra-virgin olive oil

1 garlic clove, peeled

Fine sea salt

Cook the greens in a large pot of boiling well-salted water until they have lost some of their bitterness, about 10 minutes, then drain (don't drain completely; you want some water still clinging to the greens). When the greens are cool enough to handle, chop into 2-inch pieces.

Combine the olive oil and garlic in a medium skillet over medium heat and cook until the garlic starts to turn golden (be careful not to burn the garlic), about 5 minutes. Add the greens and cook 10 minutes more, turning several times to coat evenly with oil. Season with salt to taste.

— *Serves 4*

When my mother started doing her promotional tours in the U.S., one of the dishes she loved to demonstrate was spaghetti tossed with a tangle of wild greens and fresh ricotta. I think people found this pasta so appealing because it was straightforward and real, just as my mother was with all her guests.

Spaghetti con Verdure di Campo e Ricotta
Spaghetti with Wild Greens and Ricotta

2 pounds wild greens (Swiss chard, kale, broccoli rabe, mustard greens, dandelion, spinach, arugula, and/or escarole can be substituted)

¼ cup extra-virgin olive oil

1 medium red onion, chopped

1 garlic clove, chopped

Pinch of red pepper flakes (optional)

Fine sea salt and black pepper

1 pound bucatini or spaghetti

⅓ cup finely grated pecorino, Ricotta Infornata (page 79), or ricotta salata, plus more for serving

4 ounces whole-milk ricotta, preferably sheep's milk

Cook the greens in a large pot of boiling well-salted water until they have lost some of their bitterness, about 10 minutes. Drain (don't drain completely; you want some water still clinging to the greens). When the greens are cool enough to handle, chop into 2-inch pieces.

Combine the olive oil, onion, and garlic in a large skillet and cook over medium heat until the onion is softened, about 5 minutes. Add the greens and toss to coat with the oil, then season with the red pepper flakes (if using) and salt and black pepper to taste. Cook until the greens are very tender, about 10 minutes, then remove from the heat.

Meanwhile, cook the pasta in a pot of boiling well-salted water. Reserve 1 cup of the cooking water, then drain the pasta and add it to the skillet with the greens. Cook over medium-high heat for 1 to 2 minutes, adding some or all of the reserved cooking water if the mixture is dry. Sprinkle with the grated pecorino. Serve with dollops of fresh ricotta on top and more grated cheese on the side.

— Serves 6

Even though there are seemingly endless varieties of greens and weeds one can pick and eat, Giovanna and the other workers at Regaleali will collect only some of them, looking down on greens eaten in other parts of Sicily or the world. I remember once coming back from Modica, where I had had a delicious meal based on *senapa*, a type of wild mustard green that is usually boiled and then sautéed with olive oil, garlic, and chile pepper. When I asked Giovanna if she had ever had it, she answered sharply that they don't eat such things in Vallelunga. A few years ago, my friend Niloufer visited from San Francisco and introduced me to *amaranta*, a weed that no one here would ever consider eating. I can't even describe Giovanna's and Pompeo's faces when I asked Pompeo to pick a big batch of it, which Niloufer then sautéed with ginger. This recipe is not at all Sicilian, just utterly delicious!

Amaranta Saltata con Aglio e Zenzero
Sautéed Amaranth with Ginger and Garlic

¼ cup extra-virgin olive oil

1-inch piece of ginger, peeled and finely chopped or grated

1 garlic clove, finely chopped

1½ pounds fresh amaranth leaves

Fine sea salt and black pepper

Combine the olive oil, ginger, and garlic in a large skillet and cook over medium heat, stirring occasionally, until the ginger and garlic are lightly colored and fragrant, about 2 minutes. Add the amaranth and cook, turning often to coat evenly with oil, until tender, about 15 minutes. Season with salt and pepper to taste.

— Serves 4

Amaranth flan is pure invention—I don't believe such a dish has ever occurred to a Sicilian chef or home cook before Niloufer introduced me to these greens. The result mixes high and low, monsù and peasant, gentle béchamel with a bite of the wilderness! Like any kind of wild greens, amaranth needs to be collected at the right moment, before the plant has flowered and while the leaves are still tender, not furry and tough. Swiss chard or broccoli can be substituted to make a milder version of this flan.

Flan di Amaranta
Amaranth Flan

2 pounds amaranth leaves or Swiss chard (coarse stems discarded)

2 tablespoons butter, plus more for the mold

⅓ cup all-purpose flour

1 cup whole milk

2 tablespoons finely grated Parmesan or pecorino

Pinch of nutmeg

Fine sea salt

⅔ cup whole-milk ricotta, preferably sheep's milk

3 eggs

Cook the greens in a large pot of boiling salted water until very tender but still bright green, about 8 minutes. Drain well. When the greens are cool enough to handle, squeeze all excess water out. Put the greens in a food processor and puree until very finely chopped. Leave the greens in the food processor.

Preheat the oven to 400°F. Butter a 9-inch flan mold.

Melt 2 tablespoons butter in a medium saucepan. Remove from the heat and whisk in the flour. Gradually whisk in the milk, return the sauce to the heat, and cook, stirring constantly, until very thick, about 10 minutes. Stir in the Parmesan, nutmeg, and salt to taste, then add the ricotta. Transfer the béchamel mixture to the food processor with the greens and puree until very smooth and creamy. Blend in the eggs, then spoon into the prepared flan mold.

Place the filled mold in a large baking pan and pour boiling-hot water into the pan so that it reaches halfway up the mold. Bake until just set, 30 to 40 minutes. Cool slightly, then invert onto a serving platter.

Note: For broccoli flan, reduce the flour to ¼ cup, use only 1 egg, and substitute 1½ pounds broccoli for the amaranth greens or Swiss chard.

— Serves 6

HERBS

Whenever I can buy or make a graft of a wild herb or some sort of interesting scented plant I try to find the right place for it at Case Vecchie. I like the idea of walking through the garden and encountering specific, interesting scents. Every year I travel to the extreme south of Sicily to visit specialized nurseries (people smile at this, thinking there cannot be such huge distances in Sicily, but the roads are so twisty, the landscape so different every fifty miles, that the ride across the island down to the southeastern part is actually quite a journey!). There, I find all sorts of wild, domestic, and exotic varieties of thyme, rosemary, geranium, mint, sage, lavender, and lemon verbena.

We harvest many of these herbs in the early fall and hang them in a cool spot to dry. Once they are fully dry, we crumble them to make an herb blend that we use to season all sorts of things, from the Stuffed Turkey (page 40) we make for Christmas to a much simpler roast chicken that we prepare almost once a week at the cooking school. The following recipe is not meant to be an exact guide; you should use whatever herbs and quantities you like the best.

Potpourris di Aromi di Case Vecchie
Case Vecchie Herb Blend

10 branches rosemary

4 branches sage

2 branches bay leaves (about 40 leaves)

2 branches scented geranium (the herb: leaves and flowers)

3 handfuls lemon thyme

3 handfuls orange thyme

1 handful catnip

1 large bunch oregano, preferably wild

Dried zest of 1 orange, chopped

1 tablespoon fine sea salt

Hang the herbs in a cool, dry spot to dry completely. Carefully remove the dried leaves from the branches and pulse in a food processor with the chopped orange peel until finely ground (you may have to do this in batches). Stir in the salt. Store in airtight containers.

— Makes about 4 cups

We have always raised chickens at Case Vecchie, both for meat and for their eggs. There is truly nothing comparable to the taste of a home-raised chicken, and I have seen even strict vegetarians diving into the roast chicken we make at the cooking school. When my grandmother was still alive, it was her job to look over the chickens and decide when they should be butchered. So every couple of weeks, a shipment of different-size birds was sent from Case Vecchie to her house in Palermo, where they were tested—either roasted whole or cooked as *polletto alla valdostana*, with prosciutto and cheese. When she decided the chickens had reached the perfect weight and size, they were all killed and frozen. These days, my Uncle Lucio has taken over this task and gets to decide when the crucial moment has arrived.

Pollo Arrosto al Vino con Aromi di Case Vecchie
Roast Chicken with Wine and Case Vecchie Herb Blend

1 large red onion, coarsely chopped

1 (3- to 4-pound) chicken

1 lemon, halved

1 tablespoon Case Vecchie Herb Blend (page 236)

½ teaspoon fine sea salt

¼ teaspoon black pepper

1 tablespoon extra-virgin olive oil

¾ cup white wine or freshly squeezed orange juice

Preheat the oven to 375°F. Oil a baking pan and scatter the chopped onion in the pan. Place the chicken in the pan and stuff with the lemon halves. Rub the herb blend, salt, and pepper all over the skin of the chicken. Drizzle with the olive oil. Roast the chicken until its skin is golden brown and juices run clear, about 1 hour. Toward the end of cooking, pour the wine or juice over the chicken and bake until the wine or juice evaporates. Serve the chicken with the pan juices.

— *Serves 6*

Costolette di agnello was one of my favorite dishes as a child, maybe because we got to eat the savory ribs and chops with our hands. We eat them all year round, usually roasting them in the oven, except for Pasquetta, the day after Easter, which is traditionally celebrated with a picnic, and other special occasions when we grill them outside, along with coils of fresh sausage and *stigghiole* plus plenty of Roasted Artichokes (page 107) cooking in the coals.

Costolette di Agnello
Lamb Ribs and Chops with Case Vecchie Herb Blend

2½ pounds thin-sliced lamb ribs and chops

2 garlic cloves, minced

1 tablespoon Case Vecchie Herb Blend (page 236)

1 tablespoon fine sea salt

3 tablespoons extra-virgin olive oil

Juice of 1 lemon or ½ cup white wine

Place the ribs and chops in a large, well-oiled roasting pan. Rub with the garlic, herb blend, and salt and drizzle with the olive oil. Marinate at room temperature for 1 hour.

Preheat the oven to 350°F. Bake the ribs and chops for 20 minutes. Drizzle with the lemon juice or wine and bake for 10 minutes more.

— Serves 4 to 6

Mothia's salt pans, on the western coast of Sicily, south of Trapani, are one of the most magical places on the whole island. I went there for the first time with my mother to buy some sea salt and to talk with one of the owners of the salt pans. It was September, nearly time to harvest the salt, and the basins of water were tinged with pink from all the salinity. The coastal landscape was punctuated surreally with Dutch-style windmills once used to grind the salt and hills of salt protected by neat stacks of clay roofing tiles. Pink flamingos stared at us while they waited for the right moment to start their migration to Africa. I was moved by the beauty and strangeness of it all, and since then, I always buy my salt there. (When I call for salt in a recipe, I do mean sea salt, which should be finely ground.) I like the sea salt from Mothia because it is not too salty, and it has a sort of sweetness that I find very appealing, just like this beautiful place.

When I serve the Roast Chicken or the Lamb Ribs, I often make my pan-roasted potatoes to go with them. These are the potatoes I used to make for my children when I was in a hurry, going back and forth from the house to the museum. I would boil the potatoes in the morning while we were having breakfast, then drain them and let them sit until noon when I came back to prepare lunch. At that point I roughly chopped the potatoes, covered a pan with olive oil, threw in the potatoes, sprinkled them with lots of dried oregano and a big pinch of salt, and cooked them over high heat. The key is not to fiddle with them too much; the less you move the potatoes around, the crunchier the peel gets.

Patate Saltate con Origano
Pan-Roasted Potatoes with Oregano

3 pounds potatoes

⅓ cup extra-virgin olive oil

1 tablespoon dried oregano, preferably wild

2 teaspoons fine sea salt

Cook whole potatoes in a large pot of boiling salted water until tender. Drain. When cool enough to handle, chop the unpeeled potatoes into large chunks. Heat the olive oil in a very large heavy skillet over medium-high heat, then add the potatoes. Sprinkle the potatoes with the oregano and salt and cook, turning occasionally, until golden brown and very crisp, 15 to 20 minutes (keep watch so the potatoes do not burn).

— Serves 4 to 6

Giovanni, the man who looks after

the vegetable garden, has a real talent for plants, as well as a curiosity about new varieties, recipes, and ingredients—an openness that is quite rare in remote parts of Sicily—and I appreciate that. Many mornings, he and I take a tour of the garden together, and he plays a little game with me, waiting to see if I can notice any changes he has made. When I don't, I feel rather ashamed!

Most of Giovanni's knowledge comes from his father, Pinuzzo, who actually started the garden with my mother thirty years ago. Like Pinuzzo, Giovanni is a man of many skills. He knows when the bees are ready to be moved from one place to another and when the right time is to prune this tree or harvest that vegetable. The world of grafting has no secrets for Giovanni; he has grafted lemons to grapefruit trees and almonds to apricot trees. Obviously the garden has gone through many changes since my tenure, and every time Pinuzzo comes over for a "check-up," we start talking and I literally bombard him with questions. Where and when did he prune this pomegranate tree, what is the name of this old kind of fruit, where does he think I should put the licorice plant he has promised me, and so on. With his wealth of knowledge, Giovanni has certainly followed in his father's footsteps, for which I am so grateful.

QUINCES

My mother planted many quince trees in our garden, and now that I look after the garden I can understand why. The quince is a very generous, graceful tree that doesn't require much care. Plus, it is resistant to frost, which, at about 1,800 feet above sea level, we often get at Regaleali. In April, hairy white flowers cover the tree, and come fall, it is laden with knobby, fuzzy, yellow fruits that are gorgeous to look at and delicious to eat once they have been cooked properly. We use the fruit to make quince paste, which we call *cotognata*. In Sicily we eat it just as a sweet treat, not with cheese as they do in Spain or South America with *membrillo*. My mother passed down the recipe she learned from Maria Ognibene, Giovanni's mother, who was the housekeeper at Case Vecchie many years ago. I remember my mother sending me various kinds of *cotognata* when I was living in Verona: Once it arrived very soft, other times too hard, sometimes very pale, other times dark pink. Maria was always experimenting, and the result was often moody. My mother also loved to put lots of lemon in the *cotognata* (she had a passion for lemons and would squeeze lemon juice on almost anything, even omelets, much to my father's and my disapproval!). When Giovanna arrived

at Case Vecchie, she took matters in hand and dialed down all the excess lemon and sugar, and now our *cotognata* is perfectly consistent, with a beautiful dark reddish hue and a lovely solidity.

In November, when the quinces are ripe, Giovanni collects all of them from the garden and we prepare them for boiling. Raw quinces are hard as rocks, and peeling the fruit is a workout. Then they must be boiled until tender and passed through a food mill before getting cooked again with lots of sugar. The steaming-hot mixture must be stirred constantly as it simmers and bubbles. When it has reached the right consistency and color, we pour it into decorative ceramic molds as well as shallow sheet pans to firm up. Once the *cotognata* has dried enough, I like to cut several sheet pans' worth into small rectangles and wrap them in colorful paper for my Christmas basket gifts.

Cotognata
Quince Paste

5 pounds quinces, peeled, cored, and quartered

About 4 pounds sugar

Juice of 4 lemons

Cook the quinces in a large pot of boiling water (the water needs to cover the quinces), uncovered, until tender enough to be pierced with a fork, about 30 minutes. Drain (reserve the cooking liquid if you want to make Quince Jelly, page 251).

Pass the cooked quinces through a food mill. Weigh the puree and put it back in the pot. Weigh out an equal amount of sugar and stir it into the puree. Add the lemon juice. Bring the mixture to a boil. Reduce the heat and simmer, stirring constantly. Protect your hand and arm, as the puree is very hot and will spatter. Cook until the puree is thickened, shiny, and deep pink, about 1½ hours.

Spoon the puree into shallow ceramic molds or dishes (about 1 inch deep), cover with cheesecloth, and let stand for 4 to 5 days.

When the paste begins to pull away from the sides of the molds, unmold it and invert it to dry the other side. Leave, uncovered, in a cool, dry place for up to 1 month. Cut into pieces and wrap in wax paper after that.

— Makes 5 to 6 cups

As with lemon sorbet, quince jelly was a lucky discovery. I knew that quinces were very rich in pectin, so it seemed likely that jelly could be made from the translucent pink juice left over from boiling the quince. An old friend nearly scared me off by telling tales of letting the juice strain drip by drip through a tea towel. Giovanna and I instead decided to boil down the cooking water, with some added sugar. The jelly was a success! When the mixture has reduced sufficiently, it will still seem quite liquidy, but it will firm up as it sits in the jars. The quince jelly has a marvelous color and perfume and is delicious to eat on toast or with good yogurt for breakfast.

Gelatina di Melecotogne
Quince Jelly

4 cups cooking liquid left over from   4 cups sugar
    making Quince Paste (page 250)

Strain the cooking liquid through a fine-mesh sieve, then combine with the sugar in a large saucepan and cook over medium heat, stirring, until the sugar is dissolved. Bring to a boil, then reduce to a simmer and cook, stirring frequently and skimming off any foam from the surface, until the liquid is reduced by half. Pour the hot mixture into sterilized half-pint jars, seal tightly, and turn upside down to cool. Store in a cool, dark place.

— Makes about 5 half-pint jars

OLIVES AND OLIVE OIL

The olive harvest is as big an event as the grape harvest but much less stressful. If it rains—which it often does by the end of October or beginning of November, when the olives are ready to be picked—it isn't as dramatic as it is for the grapes. Grapes are delicate and can get moldy if they get wet and the sun does not dry them quickly. Olives, on the other hand, can stay a bit longer on the tree (though not on the ground, where they get bruised and give a bad taste to the oil). Olive oil has been made forever at Regaleali, but the taste of it has vastly improved since my cousin Giuseppe imposed some guidelines, namely that the olives must be pressed on the same day that they are harvested and that our olives are the first to be processed, on absolutely clean equipment, so that no trace of an old pressing can get into our oil and give it a rancid flavor.

Over the years, the olive plantation has also become more organized, with a tidy plot of trees, mostly the Biancolilla variety, planted along one of the hills that slopes down from Case Grandi. But until a few decades ago, olives were planted randomly, wherever there was a spare hole. There are still a few small, old orchards at Regaleali that are composed the old-fashioned way, where olive trees grow among grapevines, while the vines crawl upon the figs, and the figs face an apple tree, and the apple tree shares its soil with sunflowers and dahlias. That sort of hodgepodge planting, picturesque as it is, won't do anymore, since Regaleali now produces about five thousand liters of olive oil each year.

The olives are still picked the old way. The workers spread large nets under the trees and knock down the olives with Teflon pitchforks, which don't bruise the olives or the branches. From there, the olives are carefully loaded on trucks and taken to the *oleficio* in Vallelunga, where they get pressed that same day. The olives are picked halfway between green and black, and the oil they make is sharp, with a hint of spice in it. In Vallelunga, the tradition is to fry small rounds of dough known as *vastedde* in this *olio nuovo*, and then dip them in sugar and cinnamon.

Pompeo is the olive expert at Case Vecchie, and each fall he cures the black olives and brines the green. Pompeo salts the black olives and puts them out to dry on screens in the sun, raking through them with his hands regularly so that they cure evenly. When the olives are fully black and cured, which takes about a week and a half, Pompeo rinses them and stores some in jars with olive oil, while he freezes the others as is. He packs the green olives in huge jars filled with brine, plus a few branches of wild fennel, some fresh bay leaves, and garlic cloves.

My grandmother always had a platter of green and black olives sitting on the table during our meals. Now I often offer the rosemary-scented black olives or the green olive salad before dinner with a nice glass of wine.

Olive Nere al Rosmarino e Scorzetta di Arancia
Black Olives with Rosemary and Orange Zest

1 pound oil-cured black olives

½ cup extra-virgin olive oil

2 garlic cloves, peeled and smashed

1 teaspoon coarsely chopped fresh
  rosemary leaves

1 small hot pepper, chopped

Grated zest of 1 orange

Pinch of brown sugar

Warm the olives in a medium skillet over medium heat until shiny and plump, about 5 minutes. Transfer to a bowl and stir in the olive oil, garlic, rosemary, hot pepper, orange zest, and brown sugar. Serve at room temperature.

— Makes 2 cups

Olive Verdi con Cipolla e Origano
Green Olives with Red Onion and Oregano

1 pound green olives

½ small red onion, sliced

1 celery stalk with some tender
  leaves, chopped

1 carrot, thinly sliced

1 garlic clove, minced

2 tablespoons dried oregano,
  preferably wild

1 small hot pepper, chopped

½ cup extra-virgin olive oil

2 tablespoons red or white
  wine vinegar

Rinse the olives to remove excess salt and shake them dry. Combine the olives in a bowl with the onion, celery, carrot, garlic, oregano, and hot pepper. Gently stir in the olive oil and vinegar. Serve at room temperature.

— Makes 2 cups

Focaccia is universal in Italy, and each village has its own style; but it is usually a doughy pizza stuffed or seasoned with simple things such as olives, tomatoes, or onion. We make this focaccia every time we go out for a picnic, and it's very good paired with our sun-dried tomatoes and Preserved Artichokes (page 115).

Focaccia con Olive Nere
Focaccia with Black Olives

DOUGH

3½ cups durum wheat or semolina flour

1½ tablespoons fresh compressed yeast

¾ cup water, divided

½ cup extra-virgin olive oil

½ cup white wine

1½ teaspoons fine sea salt

TOPPING

¾ cup oil-cured black olives, pitted

Leaves from 2 sprigs fresh rosemary

Fine sea salt

2 tablespoons extra-virgin olive oil

Make the dough: Mound the flour on a work surface and make a well in the center. Add the yeast to the well and start adding enough water (about ¼ cup) to dissolve the yeast, mixing with your hands. Mix in the olive oil until incorporated, then mix in the wine until incorporated, and add about ¼ cup water. Add the salt and more water if the mixture seems too dry. Knead the dough for 10 to 15 minutes (it will be quite sticky), then transfer to a large oiled bowl and let rise, covered with a towel, in a warm place for about 30 minutes.

Preheat the oven to 400°F. Press the dough into an oiled 10-inch springform pan and let rise for another 10 minutes.

Prepare the topping: Press the dough with your fingertips to make dimples in the dough. Arrange the olives in the dimples. Sprinkle with the rosemary and salt, and drizzle with the olive oil. Bake until golden, about 30 minutes.

— Serves 6 to 8

I think of Carmelo as the supergardener. He is the gardener of Case Grandi's vegetable garden, but he actually oversees Case Vecchie's garden as well. His father was a shepherd, so Carmelo also knows a lot about cheese, but I think his real passions are plants and animals. He has gotten a wild fox to take food from his hands, an act that stunned us all.

Whenever I have a question about plants, I rush to Carmelo and we consult books and photos together. He almost always knows the answer to my question, and if not, he has some good ideas. Carmelo understands the rhythms of farming and the best, most natural ways to help things grow. He tells me that no one makes good pecorino anymore because you need to work on it every week for a whole year, and who wants to go to all that trouble? He says that you must take the same approach to lettuces and vegetables, anything growing, really—and indeed, every day, you will see him in the garden, working with his hoe and gently moving the dirt around the base of the plants so that the soil can breathe properly. He is truly a very inspiring man.

Our fields have always been overpopulated with rabbits, so farmers often become hunters. In this dish, the pungent, oily taste of the black olives balances the leanness of the meat. I like to add some fresh rosemary because it goes so nicely with the wine and the onions.

Coniglio con Rosmarino e Olive Nere
Rabbit with Olives and Rosemary

½ cup extra-virgin olive oil

1 onion, finely chopped

1 (3-pound) rabbit, cut into 8 pieces

1 tablespoon *estratto* or good-quality
    sun-dried tomato paste

1½ cups white wine

1½ cups oil-cured black olives, pitted

5 sprigs fresh rosemary

1 to 2 cups warm water

Fine sea salt and black pepper

Combine the olive oil and onion in a large heavy skillet and cook over medium-high heat until golden, about 5 minutes. Add the rabbit and cook until the skin is well browned, 8 to 10 minutes. Dissolve the *estratto* in the wine. Add the wine mixture to the pan and cook, stirring frequently, until it evaporates. Stir in the olives and rosemary. Add enough water to nearly cover the meat, then simmer, covered, over medium-high heat for 30 minutes. Test the rabbit for doneness; if necessary, cook a little longer, covered, until tender. Then uncover and cook to let the water evaporate so the sauce thickens. Season with salt and pepper.

Note: This is also delicious if you add some peeled, chopped potatoes halfway through and cook with the rabbit.

— Serves 6

To imagine a Mediterranean garden without pomegranate trees is almost impossible. It is such an ancient, beautiful fruit and embodies the long journey that many ingredients made through Asia, North Africa, and the Mediterranean basin before reaching Sicily. In many ways, it is the same path followed by my super dog Monsù, whose breed—Cirneco dell'Etna—was probably imported to Sicily by the Phoenicians. The pomegranate fruits are ready in October, and they often split open under the last heat of the autumn sun, shamelessly exposing their juicy red seeds. If the fruits are not picked promptly, the birds will swoop down and feast on them. We mostly use pomegranate seeds in our green salads or on some sweet cakes; they give a lovely sweet and sour taste to foods and are just gorgeous to look at.

CAULIFLOWER AND SQUASH

Cauliflower is called *broccoli* in Sicily, and we plant it in late August so we can start eating it in October. We grow at least three different varieties at Case Vecchie: the pale green kind, which grows mainly in the western part of Sicily, the purple one known as the Etna cauliflower, and the basic white one, whose mildness I find the least interesting. I usually only plant a few dozen of them just for comparison's sake. In a market in Caltanissetta, I discovered a fourth variety, a very pale purple, like a cross between the white and the Etna cauliflowers. When I asked about it, the vendors proudly told me it was the Caltanissetta variety but couldn't tell me anything more. I hope to plant this kind very soon!

The green one is quite firm but has a very intense flavor, and when the season starts you find them piled precariously on every street corner in Palermo. They are magnificent, a dash of striking green peeking out between the cars and the rainy atmosphere of autumn. But the purple broccoli from the eastern part of Sicily is my absolute favorite. Boiled, it melts in your mouth, like eating a sweet vegetable cream. I like to serve it as a simple side dish, gently poached and seasoned with a simple dressing of olive oil, garlic, lemon juice, salt, and pepper.

One fall day, Giovanna brought me a little recipe she had clipped from the newspaper. Since we had all the ingredients on hand, we tried making these fritters right away. They were a delicious appetizer, and with a few adjustments, they have become a regular offering when green cauliflower is abundant.

Polpette di Broccoli
Green Cauliflower Fritters

1 pound green cauliflower, cut into large pieces

4 ounces smoked scamorza cheese, finely diced

3 eggs, divided

4¼ cups unseasoned dried breadcrumbs, divided, plus more for lining the tray

½ cup finely grated pecorino

1 tablespoon finely chopped fresh rosemary or sage

1 tablespoon chopped fresh flat-leaf parsley

Fine sea salt and black pepper

½ cup all-purpose flour

Vegetable oil, for frying

Cook the cauliflower in a pot of boiling salted water until tender. Drain very well, then puree in a food processor. Transfer the pureed cauliflower to a bowl, and add the scamorza, 1 egg, 1¼ cups breadcrumbs, the pecorino, rosemary, parsley, and salt and pepper to taste. Mix well. In a large shallow bowl, whisk together the remaining 2 eggs and the flour until smooth. Put the remaining 3 cups breadcrumbs in another shallow bowl. Shape the cauliflower mixture into small, bite-sized balls, and dip first in the batter and then in the breadcrumbs. Lay out on a breadcrumb-lined tray, and repeat with remaining mixture.

Heat 2 inches of oil in a large heavy skillet. Add the balls, in batches, and fry until golden brown, 2 to 3 minutes. Drain on paper towels and serve hot.

Note: To make polpette di zucca, *or a winter squash version, replace the cauliflower with 1 pound winter squash, such as butternut, pumpkin, or acorn squash. Cut the squash into large pieces, discard the seeds, and roast in a 400°F oven until tender, about 20 minutes. When the squash is cool enough to handle, peel off the skin and discard, then coarsely chop the flesh and puree in a food processor. Transfer the pureed squash to a bowl and proceed as above.*

— Serves 4

I learned how to make risotto during my time in Veneto, a place where risotto is an art. I had fun being presumptuous by adding two of the most Sicilian ingredients to a northern Italian staple. The result is excellent, since you get the creamy consistency from the cauliflower and the crispness from the crushed almonds.

Risotto con Broccoli e Mandorle
Risotto with Green Cauliflower and Almonds

¼ cup extra-virgin olive oil

1 small red onion, finely chopped

1¼ cups arborio rice

1 pound green cauliflower, steamed or boiled, then coarsely chopped

½ cup white wine

4 cups chicken or vegetable stock, heated

2 tablespoons ground toasted almonds

2 tablespoons finely grated pecorino

1 tablespoon butter

Pinch of red pepper flakes

Fine sea salt

Combine the olive oil and onion in a medium saucepan and cook over medium heat until softened, about 5 minutes. Stir in the rice and "toast" for a minute or so, or until a slight change in color occurs. Add the chopped cauliflower and cook for 1 minute. Increase the heat to medium-high, then add the wine, and cook, stirring constantly, until evaporated. Add 1 cup of the heated stock, allowing it to come to a boil, stirring constantly. When the rice has soaked up the stock, add another 1 cup stock and boil again while stirring. Once the rice has soaked up this second cup of stock, add another ½ cup (if rice is still too dry after this step, gradually add more stock, being careful to use no more than ¼ cup at a time). When the rice is plump and cooked, remove from the heat and stir in the almonds, cheese, butter, and red pepper flakes. Season with salt to taste and serve immediately.

— Serves 4

Pasta tossed with a sauce of cauliflower, pine nuts, and currants is one of those regional Sicilian dishes you find together with caponata or cassata. It is commonly called *pasta con i broccoli arriminati* (*arriminati* means mixing and seasoning, in one word). It always works because it is very easy to make. One tip: The longer you gently sauté the cauliflower with the pine nuts, currants, and *estratto*, the better it is. So take your time.

Pasta con i Broccoli Arriminati
Pasta with Cauliflower, Pine Nuts, and Currants

SAUCE

2 small heads green cauliflower (about 2 pounds), cut into 1-inch florets

⅓ cup extra-virgin olive oil

1 medium red onion, chopped

3 anchovy fillets

3 tablespoons pine nuts

3 tablespoons dried currants

1 tablespoon *estratto* or good-quality sun-dried tomato paste

1 cup white wine

Fine sea salt and black pepper

TOASTED BREADCRUMBS

¼ cup unseasoned dried breadcrumbs

1 teaspoon extra-virgin olive oil

1 tablespoon finely chopped fresh flat-leaf parsley

Pinch of ground cinnamon

1 pound perciatelli

Make the sauce: Cook the cauliflower in a large pot of boiling salted water until tender, about 10 minutes. Reserve 2 cups of the cooking water and drain. Set aside.

Combine the olive oil and onion in a large skillet and cook over medium-high heat until just golden, about 5 minutes. Add the anchovies and mash them, then stir in the pine nuts, currants, and cauliflower. Stir the *estratto* into the wine until dissolved, then add to the cauliflower with 1 cup reserved cooking water and simmer until the cauliflower is falling apart (add a bit more cooking water if mixture gets too dry). Season with salt and pepper to taste and set aside.

Make the toasted breadcrumbs: Combine the breadcrumbs and olive oil in a small skillet and cook, stirring constantly, until well toasted. Stir in the parsley and cinnamon. Set aside.

Cook the perciatelli in a large pot of boiling well-salted water. Drain and gently toss with the cauliflower sauce and the toasted breadcrumbs.

— Serves 6

My friend Patrizia Cavalli is a poet, a cook, and a perfectionist. She is a master of soufflés, but every time she makes one (and they are always delicious), she complains that it isn't as good as the last one she made. She is the one who turned me on to this recipe, though she makes it with *broccoletti*, a kind of wild mustard you find in the markets in Rome. I simply changed the *broccoletti* to our green cauliflower since it is more available in Sicily. For extra flavor, keep the water in which you have boiled the cauliflower, and cook the pasta in it. And don't forget to reserve some of the cooking liquid to moisten the sauce, if needed.

Pasta con Broccoli e Zucca
Pasta with Green Cauliflower and Squash

⅓ cup extra-virgin olive oil

1 small winter squash, such as butternut or acorn, peeled and cut into small cubes

1 garlic clove, peeled

Fine sea salt and black pepper

1 head green cauliflower, cut into small florets

1 pound orrechiette (or other small pasta that will collect the sauce)

Ricotta Infornata (page 79), finely grated

Combine the olive oil, squash, and garlic in a large skillet and cook over medium-low heat, carefully turning occasionally, until the squash is tender and golden brown, 15 to 20 minutes. Season with salt and pepper to taste. With a slotted spoon, transfer the squash to a large bowl and loosely cover to keep warm. Reserve the oil in the skillet (discard the garlic).

Cook the cauliflower in a large pot of boiling salted water for 5 minutes, then, with a slotted spoon, transfer the cauliflower to the skillet. Cook over medium heat, stirring occasionally, until browned and tender, about 10 minutes.

Meanwhile, cook the pasta in the same pot of boiling salted water. Reserve 1 cup of the cooking water, then drain the pasta and add to the bowl with the squash. Add the cauliflower to the squash and pasta and gently stir to combine, adding some of the reserved cooking water if needed. Season with salt and pepper to taste, and top with plenty of grated *ricotta infornata*.

— Serves 6 to 8

We grow several types of winter squash at Case Vecchie. We start harvesting them in September and keep them in the storage room for several months, eating them one by one. In addition to the huge ribbed gourds with a bright deep-orange pulp inside, which we call *zucca d'inverno*, we also have the big, pale green squash that look like zeppelins. This squash is only for candying, and translucent ribbons of it are used to decorate cassata. During trips to the U.S., I fell in love with butternut squash and now plant lots of it at Case Vecchie. I especially like it in this sweet and sour preparation.

Zucca in Agrodolce
Grilled Sweet and Sour Squash

2 pounds winter squash, such as butternut, peeled and sliced crosswise ⅓ inch thick

Fine sea salt

½ cup extra-virgin olive oil

1 large red onion, halved lengthwise and thinly sliced

Black pepper

¼ cup red wine vinegar

2 teaspoons sugar

Cook the sliced squash in batches on a dry grill pan (or on a grill) over medium heat, flipping when grill marks appear. Remove from the heat and arrange in a shallow baking dish. Season with salt, then cover loosely to keep warm.

Meanwhile, combine the olive oil and onion in a medium skillet and cook over medium heat until softened, about 5 minutes. Season with salt and pepper to taste. Stir in the vinegar and sugar and cook until slightly reduced and caramelized, about 5 minutes.

Spoon the onion and cooking liquid over the grilled squash, then cover the dish and let stand for 10 minutes. Carefully stir to combine ingredients and serve warm.

— Serves 6

SICILIAN PIZZAS

Making dough is always an instructive adventure. In many cases, recipes are a fragile path to follow, since a dough's mood may change depending on the weather, the flour, or even the water you are using. So basically what you need is lots of patience, self-confidence, and practice to get familiar with the process. Beginners should stick to the amounts assigned in the recipe, since one of the most common mistakes is to add water if the dough gets too stiff or to add flour if it gets too sticky and wet. When the dough becomes too stiff, it often comes from adding your liquids too quickly, without giving them time to absorb into the flour. Too sticky? You probably haven't kneaded the dough enough. I warmly suggest that you make your dough with your hands, otherwise you will never "get" how the dough should feel, and to incorporate the liquids (eggs, water, milk) and fats (oil, butter, lard) little by little, following the dough's "voice." This means keeping it soft, elastic, and moist. I once had to make a big dough in San Francisco. Semolina flour in the U.S. is much coarser than what we use in Sicily—our semolina is more similar to very fine durum wheat flour—and I was dealing with dry yeast rather than the fresh yeast that I usually use. The dough

took ages to rise. I was frantic, but I endured and gave it the time it needed to rise, and in the end I was very pleased with it. The virtues of patience!

I think that motivation for me to cook and prepare certain foods is fully psychological—through my palate I chase a universe of affection and thoughts and senses that I could never bring back otherwise. *Sfincione* is one of those palate keys. When I was a teenager, our classes took a break at 11 o'clock, and we would all run out to grab some street food. I always went for the *sfincione*— a thick Palermitan pizza topped with anchovies, onions, tomato sauce, and breadcrumbs—that a tiny man sold from his cabined Vespa (which in Sicily is called La Lapa). At that time, it cost 50 liras for a piece of *sfincione* as big as the hand of an adult man. I remember my classmates looking at me with disgust as I inhaled that greasy pizza in the middle of the street.

Well, *sfincione* is still there today. A little fleet of *sfincione* men meet early in the morning behind the cathedral of Palermo to get their allotment of *sfincione* and ride off down Palermo's streets to sell it. I hate to be nostalgic, but today's *sfincione* is not at all what it used to be. So now I make my own, chasing the memory of the one I loved during my school days.

Sfincione
Palermitan Pizza

DOUGH

2¼ cups all-purpose flour

⅓ cup durum wheat or semolina flour

1 tablespoon fresh compressed yeast

1½ teaspoons sugar

1½ teaspoons fine sea salt

1 cup warm water, or as needed

2 tablespoons extra-virgin olive oil, plus more for the pan

TOPPING

2 red onions, thinly sliced and blanched

1 cup Salsa Pronta (page 163) or good-quality tomato sauce

1 cup unseasoned dried breadcrumbs, lightly toasted

1 cup finely grated pecorino

2 tablespoons extra-virgin olive oil

6 oil-packed anchovy filets or sardines, chopped

1 teaspoon dried oregano, preferably wild

Make the dough: Combine the flours, yeast, sugar, and salt on a work surface. Start adding the water, little by little, mixing it with your hands and using a pastry scraper to incorporate the scraps. The dough should be soft and pliable. Add the olive oil and knead the dough until very smooth, 8 to 10 minutes.

Coat a deep 9-inch square baking pan with olive oil. Place the dough in the middle of the pan and stretch the dough to the sides.

Prepare the topping: In a bowl, combine the blanched onions with the tomato sauce, breadcrumbs, pecorino, 1 tablespoon olive oil, and anchovies and mix gently together. Spread over the dough and drizzle with remaining 1 tablespoon olive oil. Sprinkle with the oregano. Cover the pan and let rise in a warm place for at least 2 hours.

Preheat the oven to 350°F. Bake for about 40 minutes. Cool on a rack. Serve warm or at room temperature.

— Serves 4

Pizza is a big deal in Italy, but except for the Neapolitan and Roman pizzas, which have very clear styles, pizza in the rest of Italy is more like a bread dough or a focaccia seasoned with anything the cook has on hand. In the southeastern part of Sicily, around Siracusa, Noto, and Ragusa, they commonly call their pizzas *scaccia*, which sounds close to focaccia. These stuffed pizzas are generally filled with bits of vegetables, cheese, and meat. The following filling is a suggestion only; *scaccia* is a great way to use up leftovers.

Scaccia Ragusana
Stuffed Pizza

DOUGH

1⅓ cups durum wheat or semolina flour

1 tablespoon lard or butter

1 tablespoon fresh compressed yeast

1 egg

Pinch of fine sea salt

¼ cup lukewarm water, or as needed

2 tablespoons extra-virgin olive oil

STUFFING

⅔ cup whole-milk ricotta, preferably sheep's milk

4 ounces cooked sausage, crumbled

½ cup Salsa Pronta (page 163) or good-quality tomato sauce

2 tablespoons finely grated pecorino

Fine sea salt and black pepper

1 small eggplant, thinly sliced and fried

1 tablespoon fresh mint leaves

1 egg, beaten

1 tablespoon sesame seeds

Make the dough: Combine the flour with the lard and yeast on a work surface, then make a well in the center and add the egg and salt and start mixing them in. Start adding the water, little by little, until the dough is smooth and firm. Knead in the olive oil. Shape the dough into a ball, then cover and let rise for about 30 minutes.

Meanwhile, prepare the stuffing: Stir together the ricotta, sausage, tomato sauce, pecorino, and salt and pepper to taste in a bowl.

Preheat the oven to 400°F. Line a baking sheet with parchment paper or foil.

Roll out the dough on a floured work surface into a square about ⅛ inch thick. Lay the eggplant slices evenly over the dough, leaving a 3-inch border all around. Spread the stuffing evenly over the eggplant. Scatter mint leaves over the stuffing. Fold one edge over the stuffing, then fold over the opposite edge. Do the same with the two remaining edges, so the stuffing is completely enclosed and the pizza looks like a fat rectangle. Carefully transfer the pizza to the baking sheet. Brush the top of the dough with the egg and sprinkle with the sesame seeds. Let rise in a warm place for 20 to 30 minutes.

Bake until the dough is golden, about 35 minutes. Remove from the oven and let cool 10 minutes, wrapped in a towel, before slicing.

— Serves 8

Preheat the oven to 400°F. Line a baking sheet with parchment paper or foil.

Roll out the dough on a floured work surface into a square about ⅛ inch thick. Lay the eggplant slices evenly over the dough, leaving a 3-inch border all around. Spread the stuffing evenly over the eggplant. Scatter mint leaves over the stuffing. Fold one edge over the stuffing, then fold over the opposite edge. Do the same with the two remaining edges, so the stuffing is completely enclosed and the pizza looks like a fat rectangle. Carefully transfer the pizza to the baking sheet. Brush the top of the dough with the egg and sprinkle with the sesame seeds. Let rise in a warm place for 20 to 30 minutes.

Bake until the dough is golden, about 35 minutes. Remove from the oven and let cool 10 minutes, wrapped in a towel, before slicing.

— Serves 8

Pizzelle is similar to *gnocco fritto*, a fried bread dough that is very popular in Emilia-Romagna. But in Sicily, we don't make it as a pocket stuffed with salami or prosciutto and *stracchino*, as they do there. We simply fry the little rounds of dough, cover them with a spoonful of fresh tomato sauce and small pieces of diced provolone, and serve them as an antipasto.

Pizzelle
Fried Pizzas

1⅓ cups durum wheat or semolina flour

1½ teaspoons fresh compressed yeast

Pinch of fine sea salt

⅔ cup warm water

Vegetable oil, for frying

1 cup Salsa Pronta (page 163) or other good-quality tomato sauce, warmed

½ cup finely diced provolone

Mound the flour on a work surface and make a well in the center. Add the yeast and salt to the well and mix in the water, bit by bit (you may not need to use all of the water). Knead until the dough is smooth and pulls away easily from your hands, about 10 minutes (the dough should be very soft). Put the dough in a bowl, and let it rise, covered, in a warm place for about 1 hour.

Heat 1 inch of oil in a large skillet. With oiled hands, take a small piece of dough and shape into a small, flat circle. Drop the dough into the hot oil and fry, turning once, until golden and puffed, 1 to 2 minutes. Drain on paper towels. Repeat with the remaining dough. Spread a spoonful of warmed tomato sauce on top of each pizzelle, and top with several pieces of diced cheese. Serve hot.

— Makes about 12

GRANDFATHER GIUSEPPE

I must talk a bit more about Grandfather Giuseppe, since it is definitely due to his great appreciation of food and wine that my whole family thinks about food the way we do! One of my grandfather's most profound pleasures was planning his daily menu with my grandmother and Mario in the morning and then spending the rest of the day waiting expectantly for what was to come. While my grandfather tasted, desired, and suggested, Mario made things happen. It was a joyful, successful partnership.

The meals they created were a kind of ritual, though lunch was slightly lighter and less imposing than dinner. My grandfather always had his two-and-a-half ounces of spaghetti, not one ounce more or less, and a half bottle of wine (well, sometimes three-quarters). He drank his own wines, of course, but there was always a good selection of foreign, especially French, wines standing like little soldiers on the console of the dining room waiting their turn. He completed his meal with a seemingly endless cigar, always a Toscano. With my grandmother, who was as impatient as we were to leave the table but knew her duty was to sit smiling up until the end, we waited and talked while Grandfather puffed on his cigar until it was finished and he had snuffed it out in a bowl of water. As a child I must say it was quite a torture. Perhaps to make up for this, my grandmother always made sure that Mario made something special for each of us, dishes we would only have at my grandparents' table.

One of the easiest and most enduring things that my grandfather and his chef Mario introduced to our table was *panelle*, a kind of chickpea fritter. *Panelle* are pure street food; no one would ever eat them in a private house. But what my grandfather wanted, he got. Mario was loyal to the original street food model and made thick, soft *panelle*. Later, my mother and I came up with a different kind of *panelle*: more delicate, much crisper, and meant to be eaten like a chip. We spread the hot batter out on plates, so that the edges are a bit thinner than the centers, and when they hit the hot oil, the *panelle* puff up slightly. Their hearts stay ever-so-soft, while the edges get nice and crunchy. It is a kind of homage to the *panelle* you still find in Palermo's streets, but much sexier.

Panelle
Chickpea Fritters

2⅓ cups chickpea flour, preferably
   Sicilian

3 cups cold water

Fine sea salt and black pepper

Vegetable oil, for frying

Combine the flour, water, and a pinch of salt and pepper in a medium saucepan and whisk until smooth. Cook over medium-high heat, whisking constantly, until the mixture thickens considerably (like a very stiff polenta). Reduce the heat if necessary to keep from burning. Cook for a few more minutes, stirring with a wooden spoon, until the mixture pulls away from the sides of the pan.

Working quickly, spread the mixture with a wooden spatula onto 4 or 5 dinner plates so that it is about ¼ inch thick. Cool for 15 to 20 minutes.

When the dough is cool, loosen the edges with a small, sharp knife and peel the dough off the plates and place on a work surface, stacking one on top of another. Cut the stack into 16 wedges.

Heat 2 inches of oil in a large heavy skillet. Add the chickpea wedges in batches and fry, flipping occasionally, until golden and crisp, about 3 minutes. Drain on paper towels and sprinkle with salt. Serve hot.

— Serves 6

I especially loved the large platters of fried food that Mario prepared for family dinners, masterful arrangements of *ghineffi, arancine, timbaletti*, and *panzerotti*. I can remember the street vendor on the beach near our home in Mondello singing out, *"Arancine, sfincionelle, pizze, patatine!"* hoping to attract us with his delicacies. Unfortunately, my nanny never let me taste one of his *arancine* or any of the other goodies for fear I would lose my appetite for lunch at home. In retrospect, they probably couldn't have matched Mario's perfectly fried rice balls, but I still have that song in my ear every time I fry an *arancina*.

Arancine
Fried Rice Balls

STUFFING

2 tablespoons extra-virgin olive oil

10 ounces ground meat, half beef and half pork

1 carrot, finely chopped

1 celery stalk, finely chopped

1 onion, finely chopped

2 cups Salsa Pronta (page 163) or other good-quality tomato sauce

1 tablespoon *estratto* or good-quality sun-dried tomato paste

Fine sea salt and black pepper

RICE

2 tablespoons extra-virgin olive oil

1 small red onion, finely chopped

1½ cups arborio rice

2⅓ cups water

Pinch of saffron threads

2 heaping tablespoons finely grated Parmesan

Fine sea salt and black pepper

BATTER

¼ cup all-purpose flour

½ cup water

2 eggs

3 cups unseasoned dried breadcrumbs, plus more for lining the tray

Vegetable oil, for frying

Make the stuffing: Combine the olive oil, meat, carrot, celery, and onion in a medium saucepan and cook over medium-high heat until browned. Stir in the tomato sauce and *estratto*, reduce the heat to low, and cook until thickened, about 30 minutes. Season with salt and pepper to taste. Remove from the heat and set aside to cool.

Meanwhile, make the rice: Combine the olive oil and onion in a medium saucepan and cook over medium heat until softened, about 5 minutes. Add the rice and stir to coat with oil. Add the water and as soon as it comes to a boil, stir in the saffron, then cover, and remove from the heat. Let stand for 15 to 20 minutes, until the water is absorbed and the rice is tender. Stir in the Parmesan and salt and pepper to taste, then spread out onto a large plate to cool.

Make the batter: Whisk together the flour, water, and eggs in a large shallow bowl until the batter is smooth and creamy. Fill another shallow bowl with the breadcrumbs. Put a bowl of cold water next to you, to wet your hands now and then; this will help the rice stick together.

To assemble the rice balls, wet your hands in the cold water and fill the palm of one hand with a spoonful of rice. Cup your hand and make a hole in the middle, pushing the rice to the same thickness all around. Fill the hole with 1 small spoonful of stuffing and close your hand, enclosing the meat sauce with the rice. (Add more rice if you need to round out the ball.) Keep the hand with which you are spreading the rice wet. The ball should to be no bigger than a very small orange, from which it takes its name.

As you make them, roll the *arancine* in the batter to coat, compacting them with your hands. Then roll them in the breadcrumbs and coat; again pat them thoroughly with your hands. Place on a baking sheet that is sprinkled with breadcrumbs.

Heat 2 inches of vegetable oil in a large heavy skillet. Add the *arancine* in batches and fry, turning occasionally, until crisp and golden, 3 to 4 minutes. Drain on paper towels and serve warm.

— Makes about 15

I often made *gnocchi di semolino* for my children when I was living in Verona. It's a very soothing recipe. Not surprisingly, my grandfather loved it floating with butter, but I prefer a slightly lighter version served with tomato sauce.

Gnocchi di Semolino
Semolina Gnocchi

2 tablespoons butter, cut into small pieces, plus extra for the baking dish

4 cups whole milk

1½ cups durum wheat or semolina flour

½ cup finely grated Parmesan, divided

1 teaspoon fine sea salt

4 egg yolks

Salsa Pronta (page 163) or other good-quality tomato sauce, for serving, optional

Preheat the oven to 400°F. Lightly butter a large baking dish, as well as a baking sheet.

Warm the milk in a medium saucepan over medium heat. Gradually add the flour, stirring constantly to prevent lumps. Stir in ¼ cup Parmesan and the salt and cook, stirring constantly, until it thickens to the consistency of a thick polenta, about 10 minutes. Remove from heat, then add the egg yolks, stirring quickly to keep them from curdling. Pour the mixture out onto a buttered baking sheet, and flatten it to about 1 inch thick. Cool until very firm.

Cut the mixture into rounds with a 2-inch cookie cutter (push scraps into remaining mixture as you go) and arrange in overlapping rows in the prepared baking dish. Sprinkle with the remaining ¼ cup Parmesan and dot with 2 tablespoons butter. Bake until the tops of the gnocchi are browned, about 30 minutes. Serve plain or with tomato sauce.

— Serves 6

My father is very fond of kidneys, and Mario often prepared them for him as a special treat. Since not everyone appreciates kidneys the way my father does, I wait until there are no students at the school to prepare this dish, which I like to serve with a very simple risotto seasoned with butter and Parmesan.

Rognoni in Padella
Sautéed Kidneys

¼ cup extra-virgin olive oil

2 tablespoons butter

1 small red onion, chopped

1 pound veal kidneys

⅓ cup red or white wine

2 cups chicken stock

2 bay leaves, preferably fresh

Zest of ½ lemon

Fine sea salt and black pepper

Combine the olive oil, butter, and onion in a medium skillet and cook over medium heat until softened, about 5 minutes. Add the kidneys and cook until browned. Increase the heat to high, then add the wine and cook for about 30 seconds. Add the chicken stock and bay leaves and bring to a boil, then reduce the heat, add the lemon zest, and simmer, covered, until the sauce has reduced and the kidneys are fully cooked, about 30 minutes. Season with salt and pepper to taste.

— Serves 4

Involtini were the easiest way for poor people to stretch a thin slice of meat and make it look bigger and more satisfying. My mother loved eating *involtini di carne*, which are stuffed with a mixture of breadcrumbs, pistachios, ham, and cheese, and we often make them at the school because they are great fun to prepare.

Involtini di Carne
Meat Roll-Ups Stuffed with Ham, Cheese, and Pistachios

STUFFING

2 tablespoons extra-virgin olive oil

1 small red onion, finely chopped

4 ounces good-quality firm white sandwich bread, cut into ¼-inch cubes (about 1 cup)

4 ounces provolone, cut into tiny cubes

4 ounces prosciutto cotto (boiled ham), cut into tiny cubes

½ cup chopped fresh flat-leaf parsley

¼ cup pistachios

1 egg, beaten

Fine sea salt and black pepper

MEAT ROLLS AND SKEWERS

2 pounds veal or top round of beef, sliced ⅛ inch thick (if necessary, pound between sheets of wax paper)

About 1 pound good-quality firm white sandwich bread, cut into ½-inch-thick slices, crusts removed

About 24 bay leaves, preferably fresh

2 small red onions, cut into 1-inch wedges

½ cup extra-virgin olive oil

3 cups unseasoned dried breadcrumbs

Make the stuffing: Combine the olive oil and onion in a medium skillet and cook over medium-high heat until just golden, 2 to 3 minutes. Add the bread cubes and toss to coat with olive oil, but do not toast. Remove from the heat and cool. Add the provolone, ham, parsley, pistachios, and egg and mix well. Season with salt and pepper to taste and set aside.

Prepare the meat rolls: Put about 1 tablespoon of stuffing near the bottom of each slice of meat. Roll the meat over the stuffing, tucking in the edges to contain the filling, and roll into small sausage-like shapes. Repeat with the remaining meat and stuffing.

Cut the bread slices into rectangles about the same size as the meat rolls. Preheat the oven to 350°F and oil a large baking sheet.

Thread 2 bamboo or metal skewers (about 1 inch apart) through a meat roll. Add a bay leaf, a wedge of onion, and a piece of bread. Repeat to fill the skewers, then continue with remaining meat rolls, bay leaves, onions, and bread. Pour the olive oil into large shallow bowl and the breadcrumbs into another. Dip the skewers in the olive oil and then in the breadcrumbs, coating them lightly on all sides. Arrange the skewers on the baking sheet and bake for 20 to 25 minutes, turning once after 10 minutes. The meat should be lightly browned and the stuffing cooked through. Remove from the skewers and serve.

— Serves 6 to 8

EPILOGUE

When I joined my mother at Case Vecchie in 2005, in addition to cooking and learning my new job, I started traveling all over the island and making my way into family kitchens to observe, listen, taste, and interview as women cooked and baked. The panorama of faces, stories, methods, and ingredients that I encountered amazed me. At times, what I saw made Sicily seem more remote than ever, lost in time and space; at other times it felt as familiar as my own hands.

I remember my astonishment when I saw *biancomangiare* served as a first course at the feast of San Giuseppe. Why should this pudding—which in medieval times was a savory dish—appear in a remote Sicilian village as an introduction to a meal that included fava bean soup and sardine dishes? All of a sudden, my art studies and my new culinary discoveries seemed to join together, and I felt like I had stepped into a living kaleidoscope! I started seeing patterns everywhere: the similarities between the eighteenth-century stuccos in Palermo's churches and the intricately shaped cookies known as *nacatuli* from Lipari, the way the island's embroidery designs were echoed in its pastries. I was deeply moved watching an old woman in Lipari make her *pasta squadata*, shaping it so that it resembled the stone carvings I had seen on Neolithic monuments in Malta. Through such dishes, I saw the overlapping hand of history on Sicily's culinary traditions—the flavors and techniques of the island's many conquerors—and I realized how "old" and culturally complex so many of these food practices were.

The more I traveled through Sicily, the more I became aware of how fragile these traditions were. The women and men I talked with are very proud of their knowledge but often very lonely—they are treated by their own family like living monuments. Everyone recognizes the importance of this knowledge, but no one wants to go back to that hard life, and few young people are willing to take the time to learn, let alone master, these traditions.

And so I picked up my video camera and began to document as much as I could, in hopes of preserving a fragment of these perishable treasures. Over the last few years, I have observed men scour the hills for tiny shoots of wild asparagus and harvest lentils by hand, and I have filmed many elderly, black-dressed women as they prepared their family recipes. Through this ongoing video archive project, I have come to understand that food is never considered mere sustenance for these Sicilians, especially those in the island's small villages. Whether they are cooking in the kitchen or gathering ingredients in the fields, preparing food becomes a way to get together, to share and talk.

I take these videos with me to talks and cooking classes around the world, in the hopes that others will find as much inspiration in these time-worn hands and faces and skills as I do. I like to think that if more people know about these traditions, the less likely the traditions are to die out. But sharing these recipes and videos isn't enough. I want to convey this ancient rhythm of life, this way of experiencing the land and sharing food that is embodied by the lives of these hardworking people. My dream is for Case Vecchie and the cooking school to be a whole living organism that starts from the land, the villages, and the people and ends up on the table, blending those different moments into a whole living experience.

Homer depicted Sicily as the "garden of Hesperides," and it still is; we simply need to unveil and rediscover it. Nowadays, cooking classes at Case Vecchie no longer remain confined to the kitchen but are spread around the country, assimilating the mood, climate, colors, and perfumes of the landscape, as well as the farming and processing techniques. I want to expand the scope of the cooking school by taking guests out of the kitchen. So not only will they get to eat a delicious pasta, but they will visit the wheat fields and the pasta factory. They will help harvest the artichokes that are served with the pasta and watch a shepherd make the pecorino that is grated over the final dish. I hope that all this will give our guests a better understanding of the preciousness of the ingredients and the amount of labor behind that deceptively simple bowl of food.

"This is exactly how my grandmother used to do it." I hear this often when I am cooking, and it is a lovely compliment. The food I make these days is not "fancy" food. It is meant not to perform but to cheer. And so it should be—these are the tastes I inherited from my family and my people. It is food that tastes of the sun and the dust of the land, food that is made of love, patience, and labor.

SOURCES

AMMONIUM BICARBONATE is a leavening agent that is most often used for cookie recipes, such as Buccellati (page 46) and Taralli (page 210). Its powerful ammonia smell disappears during baking, and it leaves no aftertaste. Sometimes labeled ammonium carbonate or hartshorn, it can be found in some baking shops, gourmet markets, Fante's Kitchen Shop, and N.Y. Cake.

The ring-shaped pasta known as ANELLETTI is fundamental to making *timballo*, a baked pasta dish that is unmolded before serving. The pasta's sturdy structure makes it ideal for long cooking. The days when you could find anelletti only in Sicily have come to an end—look for it in Italian markets and Trader Joe's.

Made from ground dried garbanzo beans, CHICKPEA FLOUR is the basis for *panelle*, the quintessential Palermitan street food snack. Sicilian chickpea flour, often labeled *farina di ceci*, is more finely ground than its Indian counterpart. Look for the Sicilian flour in Italian markets, gourmet shops, and Formaggio Kitchen.

Long, pale green CUCUZZE SQUASH can grow to awesome lengths—3 feet or more. Its flesh is crisp and white, and its thin skin does not require peeling. During its late-summer season, look for it at some grocery stores, farm stands, and farmers markets, especially in areas with large Italian populations. It is available via mail order from Melissa's/World Variety Produce and Cordaro Cucuzza Plantation.

ESTRATTO, an intensely flavored tomato paste, is made by boiling, puréeing, then air-drying a huge quantity of plum tomatoes on wooden tables in a sunny place for a day or two until it has thickened to a thick, claylike paste. It is traditionally used to flavor vegetable soups and meat-based dishes. Small jars of *estratto* can be found at fine Italian markets and Market Hall Foods.

When preparing jelled desserts like bavaroise, most European cooks prefer to use GELATIN SHEETS, rather than powdered gelatin. It's difficult to convert recipes that call for sheet gelatin to a powdered equivalent, so it's worth seeking out the sheets at Fante's Kitchen Shop, N.Y. Cake, and other fine baking shops.

Unripe or GREEN WALNUTS are the basis for *nocino*, a deeply flavored liqueur spiced with cinnamon, cloves, and coriander. Mandorlino (page 151) follows the same recipe but uses GREEN ALMONDS. These unripe nuts are available for only a short window of time in the spring and early summer. Look for them at local orchards or some farmers markets. To order green walnuts by mail, contact Local Harvest. For green almonds, contact Stewart & Jasper Orchards or Earthy Delights.

LIQUID GLUCOSE is a clear syrup derived from corn or wheat starch, grape juice, or certain vegetables. It does not crystallize easily and is used to make marzipan for cassata (light corn syrup can be substituted) and gum paste. You can often find it at baking supply shops, such as N.Y. Cake.

Though many herbs are used fresh in Sicilian cooking, OREGANO is most often used in its dried form. Many Sicilian cooks like the intense, aromatic flavor of wild oregano, which grows all over the island. Dried wild oregano, which is usually harvested near Mount Etna, can be ordered from some Italian markets, Zingerman's, and Gaucho Gourmet. Cultivated Sicilian oregano, also dried and sold in bunches, can be found at most Italian markets, gourmet shops, and many supermarkets.

SEA SALT has been produced in Sicily since the time of the Phoenicians, mostly along the western coast of the island in Mothia (sometimes called Mozia) and Trapani. Look for Sicilian sea salt at gourmet food shops, Italian markets, Formaggio Kitchen, and SaltWorks.

Ricotta—which literally means "re-cooked"—is made by cooking the whey left over from making cheese. SHEEP'S MILK RICOTTA is what is most widely available and used in Sicily, but can be harder to find in the United States. Look for it at farmers markets and gourmet cheese shops.

TENERUMI are the wide, tender vines from the *cucuzze* squash, and they are sold separately at Sicilian markets. They are less commonly available in the United States, so it is best to develop a relationship with a farmer who grows *cucuzze* in order to get the greens, as well. For seeds to plant your own *cucuzze* or to mail-order fresh tenerumi, contact Cordaro Cucuzza Plantation.

VINO COTTO ("cooked wine") is grape must, or unfermented juice, that has been cooked until it has reduced a thick, dark syrup. It is often flavored with spices such as bay and clove. Vino cotto can be found at Italian markets, gourmet shops, and Buon Italia.

One of the most emblematic flavors of Sicilian cuisine, WILD FENNEL grows all over the island. You will often see cars parked on the side of the road and their drivers roaming the hills, collecting armloads of the plant. Its tender white stem and feathery fronds are prized for their deep anise flavor. Though wild fennel grows prolifically in parts of California, it is practically unknown elsewhere in the United States. Cultivated bulb fennel should not be substituted for the wild; their flavor and texture are too dissimilar. The best bet is to grow your own. Wild fennel seeds (ask for the nonbulbing variety) are available from some seed catalogs, Ohio Heirloom Seeds, and Local Harvest.

The *estratto* and marmalades that are produced at Case Vecchie, under the Anna Tasca Lanza label, are periodically available in the United States. Look for them at Boulette's Larder, Formaggio Kitchen, and Marlow & Daughters.

Tasca d'Almerita and Regaleali wines are distributed in the United States by Winebow. To find a retailer near you, check *winebow.com*.

For more information about the cooking school at Case Vecchie and Fabrizia Lanza's events, check *annatascalanza.com*.

DIRECTORY OF SOURCES

BOULETTE'S LARDER
415-399-1155, *bouletteslarder.com*

BUON ITALIA
212-633-9090, *buonitalia.com*

CORDARO CUCUZZA PLANTATION
318-255-6897, *cucuzzasquash.com*

EARTHY DELIGHTS
800-367-4709, *earthy.com*

FANTE'S KITCHEN SHOP
800-443-2683, *fantes.com*

FORMAGGIO KITCHEN
888-212-3224, *formaggiokitchen.com*

GAUCHO GOURMET
877-837-0521, *gauchogourmet.com*

LOCAL HARVEST
831-515-5602, *localharvest.org*

MARKET HALL FOODS
888-952-4005, *markethallfoods.com*

MARLOW & DAUGHTERS
718-388-5700, *marlowanddaughters.com*

MELISSA'S/WORLD VARIETY PRODUCE
800-588-0151, *melissas.com*

N.Y. CAKE
800-942-2539, *nycake.com*

OHIO HEIRLOOM SEEDS
ohioheirloomseeds.com

SALTWORKS
800-353-7258, *saltworks.us*

STEWART & JASPER ORCHARDS
877-256-6638, *www.greenalmonds.com*

TRADER JOE'S
traderjoes.com

ZINGERMAN'S
888-636-8162, *zingermans.com*

ACKNOWLEDGMENTS

This book has been an extraordinary adventure for me. I have learned so much from the people who surround me all year long at Case Vecchie: Giovanna and Pompeo Pacino, Giovanni Ognibene, Enza di Ganci, Carmelo Castiglione, Salvatore Sireci, Maurizio Cassenti, and Giuseppe Cassenti. They all warmly supported me while I took the time to write, ask many questions, and deal with my innumerable experiments. A special thanks to all the staff at the winery, especially my cousin Giuseppe Tasca and Gaetano Maccaronne, who supervised my "agricultural" notes on wine and olive oil. And I would have been lost without the careful eyes of former interns Lauren Bennett and Linda Sarris, who helped me so much with these recipes. For their unflagging support and enthusiasm, I am in debt to Diane Abrams, my editor at Sterling, and my agent David McCormick.

Kate Winslow and Guy Ambrosino are now a part of the family, and I cannot thank them enough for joining me on this lovely adventure.

Finally, I dedicate this book to my mother and father, who gave me the flavor of life.

INDEX

Note: Recipe titles in Italian are show in *italics*.

A

Aïoli, 130–131
Almonds
about, 146–149; marzipan vs. almond paste, 153–154; *pasta reale*, 153–154, 156
Almond and Pistachio Semifreddo, 158
Almond and Sage Pesto, 153
Almond Granita with Vino Cotto, 156–157
Almond Paste, 154
Almond Pudding, 88–89
Fresh Almond Milk, 159
Green Almond Liqueur, 150–151
Marzipan, 66–67
Pesto with Almonds and Fresh Tomatoes, 152
Amaranta Saltata con Aglio e Zenzero, 232
Amaranth
about: flan, 232
Amaranth Flan, 233
Sautéed Amaranth with Ginger and Garlic, 232
Amarene Incileppate, 207
Anelletti con Salsa Pronta e Ricotta, 166–167
Arancine, 284–287
Artichokes
about, 104
Artichoke Caponata, 111
Fried Artichokes, 108
Frittella with Artichokes and Fava Beans, 118
Preserved Artichokes, 114–115
Roasted Artichokes, 106–107
Stuffed Artichokes with Pine Nuts and Breadcrumbs, 109
Tagliatelle with Stewed Artichokes, 112–113
Author, background of, xi–xix
childhood in Mondello, xi
fireworks ritual, 50
grandparents and. *See* Grandparents
land and culture, xiv
learning to cook, xi–xii, xv–xvi
making life outside of Sicily, xiv
mother and, xiv–xv, xvii–xviii. *See also* Cooking school; Lanza, Anna Tasca (mother)
rediscovering home, xvi–xvii

B

Baked Cheese with Vinegar and Oregano, 59
Baked Ricotta, 78–79
Barzini, Stefania, 208
Basil, in Pesto with Almonds and Fresh Tomatoes, 152
Bavaroise al Vino Cotto, 225
Beef
Fried Rice Balls, 284–287
Meat Roll-Ups Stuffed with Ham, Cheese, and Pistachios, 290–291
Biancomangiare, 88–89
Black Olives with Rosemary and Orange Zest, 256–257
Blood Orange Salad with Red Onion and Black Olives, 24–25
Breads. *See also* Pizzas
about: Mario's brioche, 26; *muffolette*, 145
Bruschette with Olive Oil and Dried Oregano, 146
Focaccia with Black Olives, 258–259
Stuffed Brioche, 28–31
Brioche Ripiena, 28–31
Bruschetta con Olio e Origano, 146
Buccellati, 46–47

C

Canazzo di Giovanna, 187
Candied Orange Peel, 16–18
Canned Tuna, 128–129
Cannoli con Crema di Ricotta, 73
Capellini in Brodo con Ricotta, 55
Capellini in Chicken Broth with Ricotta, 55
Caponata di Carciofi, 111
Caponata di Melanzana, 182–183
Carciofi Arrosto, 106–107
Carciofi Fritti, 108
Carciofi Ripieni con Pinoli e Pangrattato, 109
Carciofi sott'Olio, 114–115
Case Vecchie
cooking school, xi, xv–xvi, xvii–xviii, 4, 35, 42, 298, 302
history and environs, xvi, xix–xx
Case Vecchie Herb Blend, 236
Cassata, 66–69
Cassatelle, 70–71
Cauliflower
about, 263
Green Cauliflower Fritters, 264–265
Pasta with Cauliflower, Pine Nuts, and Currants, 267
Pasta with Green Cauliflower and Squash, 268–269
Risotto with Green Cauliflower and Almonds, 266
Cavalli, Patrizia, 268
Cedro Lemon and Fennel Salad, 23
Cheese
about: baking ricotta, 78–79; making, 58, 62; Parmesan, 78; pecorino, 62; *primo sale* ("first salt"), 62; ricotta, 62, 78–79; sheep's milk, 58, 78; *tuma*, 58, 62

Anelletti with Tomato Sauce and Ricotta, 166–167
Baked Cheese with Vinegar and Oregano, 59
Baked Ricotta, 79
Cannoli with Ricotta Cream, 73
Meat Roll-Ups Stuffed with Ham, Cheese, and Pistachios, 290–291
pizza with. *See* Pizzas
Ravioli Stuffed with Ricotta and Mint, 74–75
Ricotta-Filled Turnovers, 70–71
Ricotta Gnocchi, 76–77
Spaghetti with Wild Greens and Ricotta, 231
Sponge Cake with Ricotta Cream and Marzipan, 66–69
Stuffed Brioche, 28–31
Cherries
  about: *amarene incileppate* cherries, 206
  Sour Cherries in Sugar Syrup, 207
Cherry Peppers Stuffed with Tuna, 132–133
Chicken. *See* Poultry
Chickpea Fritters, 280–283
Chilled Tomato Soup, 170–171
Chocolate, in Profiteroles with Chocolate and Whipped Cream, 44–45
Citrus
  about: at Case Vecchie, 4–7; citrons, 22; making preserves, 7; marmalades, 4, 7
  Blood Orange Salad with Red Onion and Black Olives, 24–25
  Candied Orange Peel, 16–18
  Cedro Lemon and Fennel Salad, 23
  Citrus-Marinated Sardines, 138
  Fried Puffs with Honey, 90–91

Lemon Cream, 19
Lemon Liqueur (*Limoncello*), 22
Lemon Marmalade, 10–11
Lemon Sorbet, 12
Lemony Knotted Cookies, 210–212
Lemony Wild Greens, 228
Orange Marmalade, 8–9
Tangerine Baskets Filled with Tangerine Jelly, 43
Tangerine Sorbet, 13
Citrus-Marinated Sardines, 138
Coffee Pudding, 207
Coniglio al Vino Cotto, 224
Coniglio con Rosmarino e Olive Nere, 261
Cookies. *See* Desserts
Cooking school, xi, xv–xvi, xvii–viii, 4, 35, 42, 298, 302
Costanza (aunt), xvii, 62, 145, 153
Costolette di Agnello Herb Blend. *See* Case Vecchie Herb Blend
Cotognata, 248–250
Crema di Limone, 19
Crostata d'Uva, 220–221
Cuddureddi, 20–21

D
Desserts
  about: cannoli, 72; for summer, 156–158, 204–211
  Almond and Pistachio Semifreddo, 158
  Almond Granita with Vino Cotto, 156–157
  Almond Pudding, 88–89
  Candied Orange Peel, 16–18
  Cannoli with Ricotta Cream, 73
  Coffee Pudding, 207
  Fig Sorbet, 204
  Filled Fig Cookies, 46–47
  Fried Puffs with Honey, 90–91
  Grape Crostata, 220–221

Lemon Sorbet, 12
Lemony Knotted Cookies, 210–212
Mulberry Sorbet, 206
Profiteroles with Chocolate and Whipped Cream, 44–45
Raised Doughnuts, 20–21
Ricotta-Filled Turnovers, 70–71
Sour Cherries in Sugar Syrup, 207
Sponge Cake with Ricotta Cream and Marzipan, 66–69
Tangerine Sorbet, 13
Watermelon Pudding, 208–209
Di Ganci, Enza, 171
Doughnuts, 20–21
Drinks
  about: herbal tea blend, 155
  Elderflower Syrup (*Sambuca*) and, 188–189
  Fresh Almond Milk, 159
  Green Almond Liqueur (*Mandorlino*), 150–151
  Lemon Liqueur (*Limoncello*), 22
Ducrot, Gloria and Enrico, 40

E
Easter celebration, 104
Eggplant
  about, 180
  Eggplant Caponata, 182–183
  Eggplant Roll-Ups, 184–185
  Giovanna's Vegetable Stew, 187
  Whole Eggplants Stewed in Tomato Sauce, 186
Eggs
  Egg Ribbons, 165
  Eggs Poached in Tomato Sauce, 164
  Fried Stuffed Eggs, 32–33
  Frittata with Fava Beans, 119

Elderflower Syrup, 188–189
Enza. *See* Di Ganci, Enza
Escarole Soup with Provolone,
53
Estratto, 172–178

F

Fall, 215–295
about: grape harvest,
217–219
Amaranth Flan, 233
Bavaroise with Vino Cotto,
225
Black Olives with Rosemary
and Orange Zest, 256–257
Case Vecchie Herb Blend,
236
Chickpea Fritters, 280–283
Focaccia with Black Olives,
258–259
Fried Pizzas, 278–279
Fried Rice Balls, 284–287
Grape Crostata, 220–221
Green Cauliflower Fritters,
264–265
Green Olives with Red
Onion and Oregano, 257
Grilled Sweet and Sour
Squash, 270–271
Lamb Ribs and Chops with
Case Vecchie Herb Blend,
238–239
Lemony Wild Greens, 228
Meat Roll-Ups Stuffed
with Ham, Cheese, and
Pistachios, 290–291
Palermitan Pizza, 274–275
Pan-Roasted Potatoes with
Oregano, 242–243
Pan-Roasted Rabbit with
Vino Cotto, 224
Pasta with Cauliflower, Pine
Nuts, and Currants, 267
Pasta with Green
Cauliflower and Squash,
268–269
Quince Jelly, 251
Quince Paste, 250
Rabbit with Olives and

Rosemary, 261
Risotto with Green
Cauliflower and Almonds,
266
Roast Chicken with Wine
and Case Vecchie Herb
Blend, 237
Sautéed Amaranth with
Ginger and Garlic, 232
Sautéed Kidneys, 289
Semolina Gnocchi, 288
Spaghetti with Wild Greens
and Ricotta, 231
Stuffed Pizza, 276–277
Wild Greens Sautéed with
Olive Oil and Garlic, 230
Fava beans. *See* Legumes
Feast of San Giuseppe, 86–88,
92, 96, 97, 171, 297
Feast of Sant'Agata, 118
Fennel
about: collecting, 92–95;
polpettine, 97; preparing
before using or freezing,
95; wild, 92–95, 96
Cedro Lemon and Fennel
Salad, 23
Pasta with Sardines, 96–97
Sautéed Wild Fennel
with Tomatoes and
Breadcrumbs, 101
Wild Fennel Fritters, 98
Wild Fennel Salad, 98–99
Figs
about: protecting from
birds, 204
Fig Sorbet, 204–205
Filled Fig Cookies, 46–47
*Finocchietto Saltato con Salsa
di Pomodoro e Pangrattato*,
101
Fiori di Zucca Fritti Ripieni,
194
Fireworks ritual, 50
Fish and seafood
about: sardines, 136–137;
swordfish, 198; tuna,
126
Canned Tuna, 128–129

Cherry Peppers Stuffed with
Tuna, 132–133
Citrus-Marinated Sardines,
138
Fried Tuna Sperm, 134
Fried Vinegar Sardines, 137
Grilled Swordfish Steaks
with Breadcrumbs,
200–201
Mint and Garlic–Stuffed
Swordfish, 198–199
My Aïoli, 130–131
Palermitan Pizza, 274–275
Pasta with Sardines, 96–97
Sardines Stuffed with
Breadcrumbs and
Currants, 139
Slow-Cooked Octopus with
Estratto and Wine, 178
Spaghetti with Tuna Roe,
135
Swordfish Roll-Ups with
Pine Nuts and Currants,
202–203
Tuna Ragù, 136
Flan di Amaranta, 233
Focaccia con Olive Nere,
258–259
Focaccia with Black Olives,
258–259
Formaggio all'Argentiera, 59
Fresh Almond Milk, 159
Fried Artichokes, 108
Fried Pizzas, 278–279
Fried Puffs with Honey,
90–91
Fried Rice Balls, 284–287
Fried Risotto Balls, 36–37
Fried Stuffed Eggs, 32–33
Fried Tuna Sperm, 134
Fried Vinegar Sardines, 137
Frittata con Fave, 119
Frittella con Carciofi e Fave,
118
Fritters
about: *panelle*, 280
Chickpea Fritters, 280–283
Green Cauliflower Fritters,
264–265

Wild Fennel Fritters, 98
Frying foods, 35

G

Galantina di Pollo, 39
Gazpacho, 170–171
Gelatina di Melecotogne, 251
Gelo di Caffè, 207
Gelo di Mellone, 208–209
Ghineffi, 36–37
Giovanna. *See* Pacino,
   Giovanna
Giovanna's Vegetable Stew, 187
Giovanni (gardener), 104,
   246–247, 250
Giuseppe (cousin), 252
Gnocchi di Ricotta, 76–77
Gnocchi di Semolino, 288
Grandparents
   author growing up and,
      xii–xiv
   Conchita (paternal
      grandmother), xii, 170
   Fabrizio (paternal
      grandfather), xii
   Franca (maternal
      grandmother), xii, xiv, 62,
      126, 152, 218, 237, 280
   Giuseppe (maternal
      grandfather), xii, xiii, 178,
      217, 280
*Granita alle Mandorle con
   Vino Cotto*, 156–157
Grapes and vino cotto
   about: harvesting grapes,
      217–219; making vino
      cotto, 222; vino cotto,
      220, 222, 224
   Bavaroise with Vino Cotto,
      225
   Grape Crostata, 220–221
   Pan-Roasted Rabbit with
      Vino Cotto, 224
Grapevines, 3, 145, 218, 220,
   224, 228, 252
Green Almond Liqueur,
   150–151
Green Cauliflower Fritters,
   264–265

Green Olives with Red Onion
   and Oregano, 257
Greens
   about: wild, 228, 232
   Amaranth Flan, 233
   Lemony Wild Greens, 228
   Sautéed Amaranth with
      Ginger and Garlic, 232
   Spaghetti with Wild Greens
      and Ricotta, 231
   Wild Greens Sautéed with
      Olive Oil and Garlic,
      230
   Zucchini Soup with Tender
      Greens, 190–191
Grilled Sweet and Sour Squash,
   270–271
Grilled Swordfish Steaks with
   Breadcrumbs, 200–201

H

The Heart of Sicily (Lanza), xv
Herbs
   about, 234; favorite tea
      blend, 155
   Case Vecchie Herb Blend,
      236
   Lamb Ribs and Chops with
      Case Vecchie Herb Blend,
      238–239
   Pan-Roasted Potatoes with
      Oregano, 242–243
   Roast Chicken with Wine
      and Case Vecchie Herb
      Blend, 237
Holidays, 26, 32, 50. *See also
   Feast references*

I

Il Mio Aïoli, 130–131
*Insalata de Finocchietto
   Selvatico*, 98–99
*Insalata di Arance, Cipolle
   Rosse e Olive Nere*, 24–25
Insalata di Cedro e Finocchio,
   23
*Insalata di Lenticchie con
   Menta e Scorzetta di Arancia*,
   120–121

Insalata di Pomodoro e Cipolle,
   168–169
Involtini di Carne, 290–291
Involtini di Melanzane,
   184–185
Involtini di Pesce Spada,
   202–203

J

Jellies and marmalades. *See*
   Sauces and spreads

K

Kale and Potato Soup with
   Fresh Mint and Parsley, 54
Kidneys, sautéed, 289
King, Niloufer Ichaporia, 190

L

Lamb
   Lamb Ribs and Chops with
      Case Vecchie Herb Blend,
      238–239
   Stewed Lamb with Fresh
      Mint, 50–51
Lanza, Anna Tasca (mother),
   xi, xiv–xv, xvii–xviii, 53, 72.
   See also Cooking school
Lanza, Venceslao (father), xv,
   42, 53, 164, 228, 289
Latte di Mandorle, 159
Lattume di Tonno Fritto, 134
Legumes
   about, 116; fava greens and
      beans, 116; lentils, 120;
      panelle, 280
   Chickpea Fritters, 280–283
   Fava Bean Soup, 90
   Frittata with Fava Beans, 119
   Frittella with Artichokes
      and Fava Beans, 118
   Lentil Salad with Mint and
      Orange Zest, 120–121
   Lentil Soup, 125
Lemon. *See* Citrus
Lentils. *See* Legumes
Limoncello, 22
Linguine con Fiori di Zucca,
   193–195

Liqueurs. *See* Drinks
Lo Menzo, Mario, xiv, xv, 26, 39, 43, 45, 50, 165, 192, 225, 280, 284, 289

M

Macco, 90
Mandorlino, 150–151
Maps, xii, xiii
Mario. *See* Lo Menzo, Mario
Marmellata di Arance, 8–9
Marmellata di Limone, 10–11
Marzipan, 66–67
Meat. *See specific meats*
Melanzane Ammuttunate, 186
Minestra di Cavolo e Patate, 54
Minestra di Scarola e Provola, 53
Minestra di Tenerumi e Cucuzze, 190–191
Mint and Garlic–Stuffed Swordfish, 198–199
Monsù cuisine, 26, 32, 184
Mothia, salt pans of, 240–241
Mousse di Fegatini di Pollo, 38
Mulberry Sorbet, 206
My Aïoli, 130–131

N

Nocino, 151

O

Octopus, slow-cooked with *estratto* and wine, 178
Ognibene, Giovanni, 104, 246–247, 250
Olive Nere al Rosmarino e Scorzetta di Arancia, 256–257
Olives and olive oil
　about, 252–255; frying foods in oil, 35; picking and processing, 252–255
　Black Olives with Rosemary and Orange Zest, 256–257
　Blood Orange Salad with Red Onion and Black Olives, 24–25
Bruschette with Olive Oil and Dried Oregano, 146
Focaccia with Black Olives, 258–259
Green Olives with Red Onion and Oregano, 257
Rabbit with Olives and Rosemary, 261
Olive Verdi con Cipolla e Origano, 257
Onions, in Tomato and Onion Salad, 168–169
Orange. *See* Citrus

P

Pacino, Giovanna, 4, 7, 15, 16, 160, 232, 248–250
Pacino, Pompeo, 15, 197, 232, 252
Palermitan Pizza, 274–275
Panelle, 280–283
Panierini di Gelatina di Mandarino, 43
Pan-Roasted Potatoes with Oregano, 242–243
Pan-Roasted Rabbit with Vino Cotto, 224
Pantelleria, 74, 145, 179
Parents. *See Lanza references*
Pasta
　Anelletti with Tomato Sauce and Ricotta, 166–167
　Capellini in Chicken Broth with Ricotta, 55
　Linguine with Squash Blossoms, 193–195
　Pasta with Cauliflower, Pine Nuts, and Currants, 267
　Pasta with Cherry Tomatoes and Sun-Dried Tomatoes, 179
　Pasta with Green Cauliflower and Squash, 268–269
　Pasta with Sardines, 96–97
　Ravioli Stuffed with Ricotta and Mint, 74–75
　Ricotta Gnocchi, 76–77
　Semolina Gnocchi, 288
Spaghetti with Tuna Roe, 135
Spaghetti with Wild Greens and Ricotta, 231
Tagliatelle with Stewed Artichokes, 112–113
Pasta all'Isolana, 179
Pasta con Broccoli e Zucca, 268–269
Pasta con i Broccoli Arriminati, 267
Pasta con le Sarde, 96–97
Pasta Reale, 154
Patate allo Zafferano, 52
Patate Saltate con Origano, 242–243
Peperoncini Ripieni, 132–133
Peppers, cherry, stuffed with tuna, 132–133
Pesce Spada Impanato, 200–201
Pesto alla Trapanese, 152
Pesto di Mandorle e Salvia, 153
Pistachios
　about: as garnish, 88; pastes, 153; poultry dishes with, 39, 40–41
　Almond and Pistachio Semifreddo, 158
　Meat Roll-Ups Stuffed with Ham, Cheese, and Pistachios, 290–291
Pizzas
　about: making dough for, 272–274; other Italian styles, 276; Sicilian, 272–274
　Fried Pizzas, 278–279
　Palermitan Pizza, 274–275
　Stuffed Pizza, 276–277
Pizzelle, 278–279
Polipetti Murati, 178
Pollo Arrosto al Vino con Aromi di Case Vecchie, 237
Polpette di Broccoli, 264–265
Polpettine di Finocchietto Selvatico, 97–98
Pomegranate, 247, 262
Pompeo. *See* Pacino, Pompeo

Pork. *See also* Prosciutto cotto
(boiled ham)
  Fried Rice Balls, 284–287
  Stuffed Turkey, 40–41
Potatoes
  about: Sicily and, 77
  Giovanna's Vegetable Stew,
    187
  Kale and Potato Soup with
    Fresh Mint and Parsley, 54
  Pan-Roasted Potatoes with
    Oregano, 242–243
  Saffron Stewed Potatoes, 52
*Potpourris di Aromi di Case
Vecchie*, 236
Poultry
  about: home-raised
    chickens, 237
  Capellini in Chicken Broth
    with Ricotta, 55
  Chicken Galantine, 39
  Chicken Liver Mousse, 38
  Roast Chicken with Wine
    and Case Vecchie Herb
    Blend, 237
  Stuffed Turkey, 40–41
Preserved Artichokes, 114–115
*Profiteroles con Cioccolato e
Panna*, 44–45
Prosciutto cotto (boiled ham)
  Meat Roll-Ups Stuffed
    with Ham, Cheese, and
    Pistachios, 290–291
  Stuffed Brioche, 28–31

Q
Quinces
  about, 248–250; *cotognata*,
    248–250
  Quince Jelly, 251
  Quince Paste, 250

R
Rabbit
  Pan-Roasted Rabbit with
    Vino Cotto, 224
  Rabbit with Olives and
    Rosemary, 261
Ragù di Tonno, 136

Raised Doughnuts, 20–21
Ravioli di Ricotta e Menta,
  74–75
Rice
  Fried Rice Balls, 284–287
  Fried Risotto Balls, 36–37
  Risotto with Green Cauli-
    flower and Almonds, 266
Ricotta. *See* Cheese
Ricotta Infornata, 78–79
*Risotto con Broccoli e
  Mandorle*, 266
Roast Chicken with Wine and
  Case Vecchie Herb Blend, 237
Roasted Artichokes, 106–107
Rognoni in Padella, 289
Rosemarie (aunt), xv, 62
Ruota di Pesce Spada, 198–199

S
Saffron Stewed Potatoes, 52
Sage, in Almond and Sage
  Pesto, 153
Salads
  about: tomatoes for, 169
  Blood Orange Salad with
    Red Onion and Black
    Olives, 24–25
  Cedro Lemon and Fennel
    Salad, 23
  Lentil Salad with Mint and
    Orange Zest, 120–121
  Tomato and Onion Salad,
    168–169
  Wild Fennel Salad, 98–99
Salsa Pronta, 162–164
Salt pans, of Mothia, 240–241
Salvatore, 92, 110
Sambuca, 188–189
Sarde a Beccafico, 139
Sarde Allinguate, 137
Sarde Marinate, 138
Sardines. *See* Fish and seafood
Sauces and spreads
  about, 4, 7
  Almond and Sage Pesto,
    153
  Lemon Marmalade, 10–11
  My Aïoli, 130–131

Orange Marmalade, 8–9
  Pesto with Almonds and
    Fresh Tomatoes, 152
  Quince Jelly, 251
  Quince Paste, 250
  Tomato Sauce, 162–164
  Tuna Ragù, 136
Sautéed Amaranth with Ginger
  and Garlic, 232
Sautéed Kidneys, 289
Sautéed Wild Fennel with
  Tomatoes and Breadcrumbs,
  101
Scaccia Ragusana, 276–277
Scorzette di Arancia, 16–18
*Semifreddo di Mandorle e
  Pistacchio*, 158
Semolina Gnocchi, 288
Sfince di San Giuseppe, 90–91
Sfincione, 274–275
Sheep's milk cheese, 58. *See
  also* Cheese
Slow-Cooked Octopus with
  Estratto and Wine, 178
Sorbetto al Limone, 12
Sorbetto al Mandarino, 13
Sorbetto di Fichi, 204–205
Sorbetto di Gelsi Neri, 206
Soups and stews
  Chilled Tomato Soup, 170
  Escarole Soup with
    Provolone, 53
  Fava Bean Soup, 90
  Giovanna's Vegetable Stew,
    187
  Kale and Potato Soup with
    Fresh Mint and Parsley, 54
  Lentil Soup, 125
  Zucchini Soup with Tender
    Greens, 190–191
  Zucchini Stewed in Tomato
    Sauce, 192
Sources, 300–302
Sour Cherries in Sugar Syrup,
  207
*Spaghetti con Uova di Tonno
  Fresche*, 135
*Spaghetti con Verdure di
  Campo e Ricotta*, 231

Spezzatino di Agnello alla Menta, 50–51
Sponge Cake with Ricotta Cream and Marzipan, 66–69
Spring, 83–141
    about: Easter celebration, 104; feast of San Giuseppe, 86–88, 92, 96, 97, 171, 297; in Sicily, 85
    Almond Pudding, 88–89
    Artichoke Caponata, 111
    Canned Tuna, 128–129
    Cherry Peppers Stuffed with Tuna, 132–133
    Citrus-Marinated Sardines, 138
    Fava Bean Soup, 90
    Fried Artichokes, 108
    Fried Puffs with Honey, 90–91
    Fried Tuna Sperm, 134
    Fried Vinegar Sardines, 137
    Frittata with Fava Beans, 119
    Frittella with Artichokes and Fava Beans, 118
    Lentil Salad with Mint and Orange Zest, 120–121
    Lentil Soup, 125
    My Aïoli, 130–131
    Pasta with Sardines, 96–97
    Preserved Artichokes, 114–115
    Roasted Artichokes, 106–107
    Sardines Stuffed with Breadcrumbs and Currants, 139
    Sautéed Wild Fennel with Tomatoes and Breadcrumbs, 101
    Spaghetti with Tuna Roe, 135
    Stuffed Artichokes with Pine Nuts and Breadcrumbs, 109
    Tagliatelle with Stewed Artichokes, 112–113
    Tuna Ragù, 136
    Wild Fennel Fritters, 98

Wild Fennel Salad, 98–99
Squash. *See also* Zucchini
    about: harvesting, 270; types of, 270
    Grilled Sweet and Sour Squash, 270–271
    Pasta with Green Cauliflower and Squash, 268–269
Stewed Lamb with Fresh Mint, 50–51
Stuffed Artichokes with Pine Nuts and Breadcrumbs, 109
Stuffed Brioche, 28–31
Stuffed Fried Squash Blossoms, 194
Stuffed Pizza, 276–277
Stuffed Turkey, 40–41
Summer, 143–213
    about: desserts for, 156–158, 204–211; in Sicily, 145
    Almond and Pistachio Semifreddo, 158
    Almond and Sage Pesto, 153
    Almond Granita with Vino Cotto, 156–157
    Almond Paste, 154
    Anelletti with Tomato Sauce and Ricotta, 166–167
    Bruschette with Olive Oil and Dried Oregano, 146
    Chilled Tomato Soup, 170–171
    Eggplant Caponata, 182–183
    Eggplant Roll-Ups, 184–185
    Egg Ribbons, 165
    Eggs Poached in Tomato Sauce, 164
    Elderflower Syrup, 188–189
    Fig Sorbet, 204–205
    Fresh Almond Milk, 159
    Giovanna's Vegetable Stew, 187
    Green Almond Liqueur, 150–151
    Grilled Swordfish Steaks with Breadcrumbs, 200–201

Lemony Knotted Cookies, 210–212
Linguine with Squash Blossoms, 193–195
Mint and Garlic–Stuffed Swordfish, 198–199
Mulberry Sorbet, 206
Pasta with Cherry Tomatoes and Sun-Dried Tomatoes, 179
Pesto with Almonds and Fresh Tomatoes, 152
Slow-Cooked Octopus with Estratto and Wine, 178
Sour Cherries in Sugar Syrup, 207
Stuffed Fried Squash Blossoms, 194
Swordfish Roll-Ups with Pine Nuts and Currants, 202–203
Tomato and Onion Salad, 168–169
Tomato Sauce, 162–164
Watermelon Pudding, 208–209
Whole Eggplants Stewed in Tomato Sauce, 186
Zucchini Soup with Tender Greens, 190–191
Zucchini Stewed in Tomato Sauce, 192
Swordfish
    about, 198; involtini, 200
    Grilled Swordfish Steaks with Breadcrumbs, 200–201
    Mint and Garlic–Stuffed Swordfish, 198–199
    Swordfish Roll-Ups with Pine Nuts and Currants, 202–203

T

Tacchino Ripieno, 40–41
Tagliatelle con Carciofi, 112–113
Tangerine. *See* Citrus
Tanis, David, 19

Taralli, 210–212
Tea, herb, 155
Tomatoes
  about, 160; paste (*estratto*),
    172–178; Roma, 160; for
    salads, 169; for sauces,
    160
  Anelletti with Tomato Sauce
    and Ricotta, 166–167
  Chilled Tomato Soup, 170
  Egg Ribbons, 165
  Eggs Poached in Tomato
    Sauce, 164
  Pasta with Cherry Tomatoes
    and Sun-Dried Tomatoes,
    179
  Pesto with Almonds and
    Fresh Tomatoes, 152
  pizza with. *See* Pizzas
  Slow-Cooked Octopus with
    Estratto and Wine, 178
  Tomato and Onion Salad,
    168–169
  Tomato Sauce, 162–164
  Zucchini Stewed in Tomato
    Sauce, 192
Tonno sott'Olio, 128–129
Traditions of Sicily, fragility of,
  297–298
Trees, pruning, 206
Tuna, 132–133
  about, 126
  Canned Tuna, 128–129
  Fried Tuna Sperm, 134
  Spaghetti with Tuna Roe,
    135
  Tuna Ragù, 136
Turkey. *See* Poultry

U

Uova alla Monacale, 32–33
Uova alla Vastasa, 164
Uova a Trippa, 165

V

Veal
  Meat Roll-Ups Stuffed
    with Ham, Cheese, and
    Pistachios, 290–291

Sautéed Kidneys, 289
Stuffed Turkey, 40–41
*Verdure di Campo con Olio e
  Limone*, 228
*Verdura di Campo Saltata con
  Olio e Aglio*, 230
Vinegar, wine, 100
Vino cotto. *See* Grapes and vino
  cotto

W

Watermelon Pudding, 208–209
Whole Eggplants Stewed in
  Tomato Sauce, 186
Wild fennel. *See* Fennel
Wild greens. *See* Greens
Winery, 217–219, 222. *See also*
  Grapes and vino cotto
Wine vinegar, 100
Winter, 1–81
  about: holidays, 26, 32, 50;
    in Sicily, 3
  Baked Cheese with Vinegar
    and Oregano, 59
  Baked Ricotta, 78–79
  Blood Orange Salad with
    Red Onion and Black
    Olives, 24–25
  Candied Orange Peel, 16–18
  Cannoli with Ricotta
    Cream, 73
  Capellini in Chicken Broth
    with Ricotta, 55
  Cedro Lemon and Fennel
    Salad, 23
  Chicken Galantine, 39
  Chicken Liver Mousse, 38
  Escarole Soup with
    Provolone, 53
  Filled Fig Cookies, 46–47
  Fried Risotto Balls, 36–37
  Fried Stuffed Eggs, 32–33
  Kale and Potato Soup with
    Fresh Mint and Parsley,
    54
  Lemon Cream, 19
  Lemon Liqueur
    (*Limoncello*), 22
  Lemon Marmalade, 10–11

Lemon Sorbet, 12
Orange Marmalade, 8–9
Profiteroles with Chocolate
  and Whipped Cream,
  44–45
Raised Doughnuts, 20–21
Ravioli Stuffed with Ricotta
  and Mint, 74–75
Ricotta-Filled Turnovers,
  70–71
Ricotta Gnocchi, 76–77
Saffron Stewed Potatoes, 52
Sponge Cake with Ricotta
  Cream and Marzipan,
  66–69
Stewed Lamb with Fresh
  Mint, 50–51
Stuffed Brioche, 28–31
Stuffed Turkey, 40–41
Tangerine Baskets Filled
  with Tangerine Jelly, 43
Tangerine Sorbet, 13

Z

Zucca in Agrodolce, 270–271
Zucchine a Spezzatino, 192
Zucchini
  about: blossoms, 193,
    194–195
  Linguine with Squash
    Blossoms, 193–195
  Stuffed Fried Squash
    Blossoms, 196
  Zucchini Soup with Tender
    Greens, 190–191
  Zucchini Stewed in Tomato
    Sauce, 192
Zuppa di Lenticchie, 125

STERLING EPICURE
New York

An Imprint of Sterling Publishing
387 Park Avenue South
New York, NY 10016

**Art direction and design by
Chris Thompson and Yeon Kim**

ISBN 978-1-4027-8783-6

Library of Congress Cataloging-in-Publication Data

Lanza, Fabrizia.
  Coming home to Sicily / by Fabrizia Lanza with Kate Winslow.
     p. cm.
   ISBN 978-1-4027-8783-6 (hardback) -- ISBN 978-1-4027-9390-5 (ebook)
 1. Cooking, Italian--Sicilian style. I. Winslow, Kate. II. Title.
 TX723.2.S55L354 2012
 641.5945--dc23
                           2012007975

Distributed in Canada by Sterling Publishing
$^{c}/_{o}$ Canadian Manda Group, 165 Dufferin Street
Toronto, Ontario, Canada M6K 3H6
Distributed in the United Kingdom by GMC Distribution Services
Castle Place, 166 High Street, Lewes, East Sussex, England BN7 1XU
Distributed in Australia by Capricorn Link (Australia) Pty. Ltd.
P.O. Box 704, Windsor, NSW 2756, Australia

For information about custom editions, special sales, and premium and corporate purchases, please
contact Sterling Special Sales at 800-805-5489 or specialsales@sterlingpublishing.com.

Manufactured in China

2 4 6 8 10 9 7 5 3 1

www.sterlingpublishing.com